This book belongs to

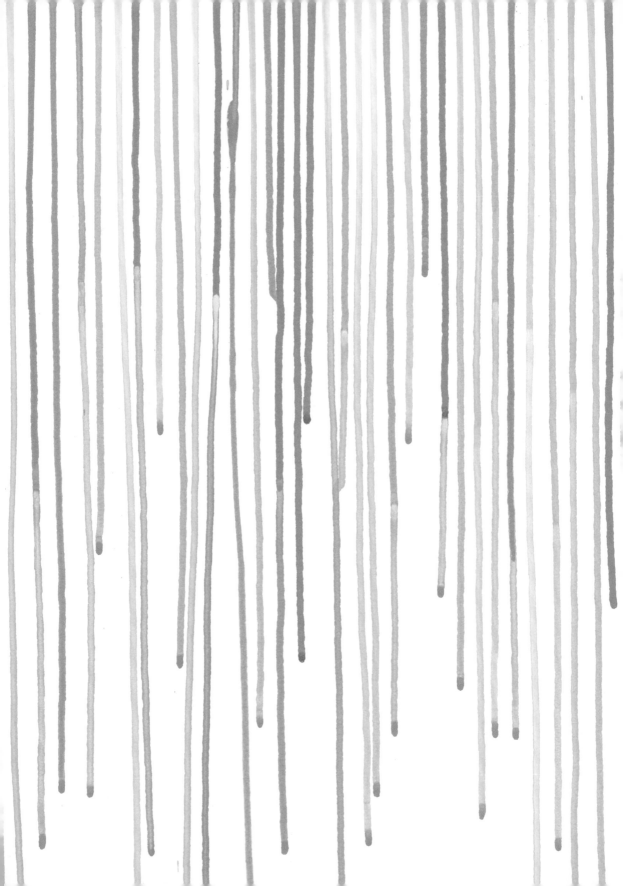

SPLENDID ICE CREAMS
AT HOME

jeni's
SPLENDID ICE CREAMS
AT HOME

Jeni Britton Bauer

ARTISAN

NEW YORK

Published by Artisan
A division of Workman Publishing Company, Inc.
225 Varick Street
New York, NY 10014-4381
artisanbooks.com

Published simultaneously in Canada by Thomas Allen & Son, Limited

Library of Congress Cataloging-in-Publication Data

Bauer, Jeni Britton.
Jeni's splendid ice creams at home / Jeni Britton Bauer.
p. cm.
ISBN 978-1-57965-436-8
1. Ice cream, ices, etc. I. Title. II. Title: Splendid ice creams.
TX795.B38 2011
641.8'62—dc22   2010039453

Chamomile illustration on pages 25 and 26 by Sally MacLeod

Printed in Singapore

10 9 8

CONTENTS

A PROMISE

Artisan American ice cream is made with ingredients that shine. It has flavor that's full of personality and it's sturdy enough to be scooped into a cone and savored on even the hottest days of the year. It's high in butterfat and low in air and, most important, it is *delicious*.

● ● ● ● ●

These recipes are as much about flavor and finish as they are about texture and consistency. I have never been a fan of "homemade" ice cream. It's usually icy, goopy, soupy, crumbly, eggy, gritty, and too buttery. So, a few years ago I set out to try to create a better ice cream recipe for home kitchens. And here it is.

Home cooks, the ice creams that you will create with this book (and readily available equipment) will make you the star of your dinner party, the talk of the neighborhood, and the hero at family holidays. Restaurant chefs, I know how difficult making ice cream in a hot kitchen is. My recipe is sturdy enough for you to create endless flavor variations that will last through

more than one shift (and even more than one day). Need a small-batch of goat cheese ice cream to accompany your roasted sour cherries? Perhaps a splendid single-origin dark chocolate ice cream to serve with a satsuma orange soufflé? Or a caramelized white chocolate ice cream to go with your warm baby banana kataiti? They're all right here!

Every recipe in this book was created and tested over and over again using only home equipment. I have included specific information about equipment, ingredients, and technique so you will be armed with everything it takes to make the most splendid ice cream you have ever tasted.

MY STORY

I started making ice cream in 1996, when I was twenty-two years old and had pink hair and lots of ideas and enthusiasm, but little business acumen. I opened my first shop, called Scream, in the North Market, a 175-year-old public market located just north of downtown Columbus, Ohio. This wonderful old building with a rich community history provided endless inspirations for new flavors. The forty-plus merchants bustling below the enormous roof were selling local produce, exotic spices, and exquisite chocolates, cheeses, and wines—the best the world had to offer—all of which went into my ice creams. I spent years perfecting my ice cream recipes in my North Market shop. Now we dish up our lovely ice creams every day in seven (and counting) scoop shops in the Columbus area, where we also serve sundaes, baked Alaska pies, cakes, and ice cream sandwiches—all handmade, from cow to cone, in our ever-expanding production kitchen.

• • • • •

How did I arrive at ice cream? The more important question is, how did I discover flavor? It was that discovery—flavor—that led me to ice cream.

Throughout high school and into college, I worked in a rustic French bakery called La Châtelaine in Upper Arlington, Ohio. There, in accordance with Old World French tradition, everything was made from scratch. Everyone in the bustling kitchen spoke French, from the Lyonnaise and Parisian pastry chefs to the Senegalese prep cooks and dishwashers. It was there that I learned to enjoy honest flavor, in the pastries made with real ingredients such as fresh berries, real butter, and vanilla beans—and less sugar than the American sweets I had grown up with.

As I peered over the shoulders of chefs filling éclairs, napoleons, and tarts with pastry cream, or twisting fresh croissants into countless configurations, each day in the kitchen brought new adventures in flavor and technique. I learned many valuable lessons there over the years. I watched the owners tackle the myriad challenges associated with operating a successful business. I learned the importance of food safety and standards of employee safety, how to successfully manage a kitchen staff, and how to order ingredients and maintain a working inventory. Such details, unglamorous as they are, are the foundation of every business, which will either support it or cause it to crumble to the ground. You may have the most delicious and innovative product out there, but without a loyal and hardworking staff who knows the value of consistency and how to crank it out the same way day after day, your business will be doomed from the beginning—a lesson I encountered more than once in my career.

I savored each moment in the bakery and I worked as much as I could through high school and in college. In time, inspired by what I saw in the kitchen and read about in cookbooks, and beginning to think about pastry school, I started to make my own sweets at home. A student of French art, I was obsessed with all things Gallic. But I also felt a strong desire to connect to my Midwestern roots. I loved the desserts from Trefzger's, a bakery in my first hometown, Peoria, Illinois. Their sweets had none of the sophistication of those lovely French tarts, but the extra-large thumbprint cookies with their sugar-bomb, pop-colored icing; Danishes with maple walnut frosting or starch-heavy fruit topping; pies of every variety; and sweetly decorated domed cakes had their own brand of deliciousness sliced out of the American Midwest. So, I thought, why not start my own American-style bakery using a few of the French techniques that I had been practicing? I began with cakes, pies, and puddings, experimenting in my small apartment kitchen. Yet I can't say that I was encouraged by the results. There just seemed to be something missing in the whole experience for me.

Then one day, I turned my attention to ice cream and something special happened. My first venture into ice cream making was the simple addition of essential oil of cayenne to store-bought chocolate ice cream. I served it at a party and my guests went crazy: It's cold! It's hot! They couldn't get enough.

After that, there was no turning back. I couldn't wait to make my first batch of homemade ice cream. From the French I had learned about salted caramel, the best and darkest chocolate, and French-style Plugra butter. From our farmers' market and my own family's gardens came honey, herbs, and fruits at the peak of flavor. Everywhere I looked, there were glorious opportunities for flavor exploration, and I used them all to come up with exciting and bold ice cream flavors. I received encouragement from local chefs and from epicurean friends.

Six months after my first explorations, I jumped into business with a friend. It was August 1996. But boy, did I have a lot to learn. We called our shop Scream. I made our ice creams in a little two-gallon batch freezer in our tiny space in the North Market. I made every ice cream and served nearly every single customer myself, and there are some good things to be said about that. Many of my early customers have remained my most enthusiastic and loyal supporters and friends. They've been with me from the early years of experimentation, and have suffered my failures, mourned my first shop's demise, and celebrated my return!

Working alongside expert food purveyors and interacting with inquisitive customers from around the world, I was never short on ideas or optimism. Slowly the ice creams got better and better as I found my rhythm. But I needed more than just a great product. I immersed myself in learning the intricacies of operating a successful business. I was a former art major with a passion for making ice cream. Running a business was a completely different animal, as foreign to my consciousness as Old Latin. So I learned from what I saw every day all around me. I learned about customer service from those merchants at the market who were particularly good at it, the ones who had lines of returning customers day after day.

I also read every book I could get my hands on about the science of making ice cream. Understanding the science behind the process, I learned, led to better ice creams and greater freedom with ingredients. I reached out to people in the dairy science department at Ohio State University, who led me to other scientists and technicians. Eventually I took the famous Ice Cream Short Course at Penn State, which crystallized all that I had learned over the years and put it all into perspective for me. I learned to see ice cream as proteins, sugars, butterfat, air, and a few other equally nonsexy components interacting in specific ways, each having its own little task, depending on how it is treated, whether singularly or in combination with other ingredients. I totally geeked-out on the process of making ice cream and slowly unlocked its mysteries.

The hardest lesson I learned at Scream was that it takes more than one person behind the counter to run a business, no matter how well intentioned that person might be, no matter how enthusiastic or inspired or dedicated to making it a success. At the beginning of my journey, I had convinced a friend to go into business with me. It was not a match made in heaven, and eventually I just had to let it go.

After we closed Scream, I was more inspired than ever to create an ice cream business that was intimately tied to our community, that contributed to it meaningfully, that both satisfied my need for change and exploration and offered enough

consistency to be sustainable as a business, drawing people back time and time again.

I was determined to save for a stainless steel commercial countertop ice cream machine from Italy that cost $1,200. It might as well have cost $12 million. But I never doubted that I would be back in business somehow—no matter how down-and-out it all seemed at that moment.

I took my mind off ice cream by diving into the challenging task of making croissants at the French bakery I'd worked for before, and for the next year I made croissants in a cloistered corner of the bakery, thousands per week. I made them from scratch in nontraditional shapes and used all sorts of fillings. It was the most difficult job I have ever had. Humidity, barometric pressure, and the phases of the moon all affected how the croissants behaved. No day was shorter than 10 hours. The end of the day was when all the croissants were made, not a moment before. But there were many lessons that I am proud to have learned in that kitchen and that have served me well since.

After the year at the bakery, I began working for a wonderful family—the Wrights. I became very close to them and told them about Scream and my business plan that was beginning to come together. I felt that if they could just try my Salty Caramel or Basil Honey Pine Nut, or my El Rey Single-Origin Chocolate Ice Cream, they might invest in the business. But I couldn't save enough money to buy the Italian ice cream machine I needed to prove my point, so I couldn't test the supposition.

Enter Charly: wonderful, funny, erudite, handsome, quirky Charly. A couple of years after he and I had gotten together, we were living in an old townhouse in the Short North, a reclaimed walkable city neighborhood with locally owned galleries, shops, eateries, and great bars. When Charly came home one night in December 2001 with the Italian ice cream machine that I had dreamed of buying, I knew that everything was going to work out. I knew that I would get back into business and that Charly and I were embarking on this ice cream adventure, for better or worse, together. I was elated. And the fact that he had faith in my ideas was a powerful encouragement. It all made me work even harder.

I decided to throw a big party, and I canvassed the North Market with my hand-carved block-printed invitations, giving one to every recognizable face. The turnout was amazing, especially considering that it was one of the coldest nights of the year. More than one hundred people came, including many of my old customers. The Wrights made it too, all five of them. It was a night of endless ice cream scooping from the small chest freezer in our dining room. And the reception my ice cream received was the final confirmation I needed to get back into the business!

There were some special guests at that party. Tom Bauer, Charly's brother, was in from Nashville for the holidays and he celebrated all things ice cream with us, never suspecting that he would shortly be moving up to Columbus to become a partner in our business. Our "attorney friend" John Lowe was also there. It's been ten years since that party. Tom has built our home delivery and online business beyond anything we ever dreamed of. Early on, John structured our LLC for us in exchange for a pint of ice cream and a beer. Seven years later, he was an executive with General Electric when Charly and I called him late one night and said, "Come to Columbus and be our CEO." There are lucky breaks in every success story—this group of people coming together is ours.

It wasn't long after the party that I was creating ice creams in my home kitchen and selling them out the door. Charly often found his Saturday afternoon television soccer games interrupted by a knock on the door from an eager customer there to make an ice cream

pickup while I was at work. I made different ice creams each week and packaged them in biodegradable boxes: Coriander Raspberry, Cherry Lambic, Bacon Praline (inspired by Charly's favorite breakfast, salty caramel ice cream covered in hot bacon), and many pints of Salty Caramel.

And for two months, I spent every free hour on my business plan. When I showed my plan to the Wrights, they were impressed. In fact, they offered me money to start the company. They also offered great advice. "Don't take it. If I give you money," Jay Wright said, "then I will want something back. Find a way to do it on your own. The money will always be here for you—think of it as a rainy day fund." Defeated again, I sobbed all the way back to Charly to tell him. I knew Jay was right, but I was at a loss.

That's when Charly decided to get involved. Charly is the yin to my yang. He is not like me—he doesn't just jump into things and take unnecessary risks—he is a very thoughtful, logical person. Yet partnering with me must have often crossed his mind during the year while I was struggling to find a way back in. He made the decision to join me, and we drew up another business plan that had us opening in the spring of 2002, but the bank was not very cooperative. We had to go back at least three times before finally getting our small loan just for the equipment. Two weeks after the loan came through, Jeni's Splendid Ice Creams opened for business, in late November, with a brand-new Italian gelato machine and two huge, shiny dipping cabinets—all the equipment needed to make beautiful ice creams right in front of our customers.

This time around I did things very differently. I bought two dipping cabinets, one for signature flavors (such as Salty Caramel, which repeat customers asked for every day, and that I had never offered with any consistency in the previous business), and one for seasonal flavors. These were made with ingredients that reflected the market on any given day. In the summer, I shopped at the farmers' market every Saturday and made flavors like Strawberry Buttermilk, Cucumber Crème Fraîche, and Backyard Mint. For the holidays, I bought Saigon cinnamon, Chinese 5-spice powder, and spicebush berries from the spice merchant; Gorgonzola and mascarpone from the cheese guy; and wines from the wine merchant to make ice creams that were warm and festive for winter celebrations. And during the slow winter months, I was inspired by other merchants to make Truffle Ice Cream, from the chocolatier's display; Butterscotch Cacao Nib (originally a pudding), from Amy the baker; Brown Bread and Treacle, from the Irish guys; Sweet Curry Ice Cream, from Raj and Billan at Flavors of India; and Pomegranate Molasses, from the Lebanese eatery. If it was in the market, I tried it. Occasionally I even made ice creams or sorbets with meats or fish: Smoked Salmon and Cucumber Sherbet, Raspberry with Veal Demi-glace Sauce, and our very popular Bacon Praline, made with Bluescreek Farms bacon and brown sugar. The merchants were glad to have me back for a second go at it, and I was grateful for the opportunity. It was the finest culinary adventure a person could have, and I relished every moment.

At Scream, I'd been a quirky pink-haired twenty-two-year-old art student. This time my hair was its natural brown and cut very short, and I wore a starched white shirt and apron every day to convey the image of a professional shopkeeper—it was like putting on a costume, and it helped me find myself. I'd resisted calling the business Jeni's at first because I thought it was too boring, but the Wrights encouraged me. They said, "All of your customers already know your ice cream as Jeni's and they're going to refer to it that way anyway." So I took their advice, and it didn't take long for me to realize the wisdom of that decision. When I was exhausted, all I wanted was a hot bath and a glass of wine; when I was tempted to open up without Salty Caramel in

Ice Cream Social

1 2 2 9 0 1

Ice Cream
Sherbet
Gelato

All
Night
Long

Bring
Wine,
Spirits

At Jeni's
95 E. First Ave #2
291-6157
7:00pm

order to allow myself to sleep in an extra hour, all I had to do was remember the fluttering paper sign hung above our business: Jeni's Splendid Ice Creams. Each night, when I got home after a twelve- to eighteen-hour shift, I was exhausted but still excited about doing it all again. That excitement continues for me to this day.

The day we opened in November 2002 was Michigan–Ohio State football game Saturday. In Columbus, that means that everyone is watching the Buckeyes play the Wolverines. Everyone. The whole town comes to a screeching halt. So we figured it would be a fine day to open. It would be a good way to ease into the coming chaos of the holidays and test the waters. A nice, quiet day selling the odd cone to one of the few Columbus residents not afflicted with Buckeye fever. We didn't have employees yet, but we figured that was okay, considering we didn't really expect anyone to show up anyway. But we had gotten the word out to some of our fans, and much to our surprise and delight, customers were lined up all day long. I can't remember how much money we made, but it seemed like a lot—especially since we were expecting to not even cover our expenses. We were exhilarated.

Today at Jeni's Splendid Ice Creams, that excitement is visceral. Everything is still made by hand, by sight, and in-house, from our ice creams to our seasonal store décor and graphic design. We handwrite the name of the ice cream on every pint (even on days when we pack 4,000 pints), as we have done since we began. The labels are our signature. We don't follow traditional rules or philosophies. Our company is based on a new model: one built around transparency and relationships. And we have built a community around our ice cream that brings many people together: our customers; our local and international farmers; our suppliers, like Askinosie Chocolate or Barley's Brewing Company; and all our employees: the kitchen team, our in-house art department, writers, and photographers. In every way, our business is based on a creative new model, and none of the old rules apply. Just the way I like it.

THE QUICK TAKE

So you have an idea of what to do before jumping in, here's an overview of the four steps you'll take to make any ice cream flavor in this book.

• • • • ●

24 HOURS BEFORE you want to make the ice cream, wash the canister, dry it well, and place it in the coldest part of the freezer. Do not remove it until you are ready to pour the chilled cream into it.

THE STEPS

PREP THREE BOWLS In a small bowl, mix about 2 tablespoons of milk with the cornstarch to make a slurry. In a medium bowl, add the salt and room-temperature cream cheese and whip all the bumps out. In a large bowl, make an ice bath (heavy on the ice) and set aside.

ADVANCE PREP

Some ice creams will call for ingredients that must be made in advance. Recipes for roasted nuts, sauces, candies, and cakes can be found in Basics (page 191). Have these components chilled and ready to go before beginning the process.

Frozen yogurts require the advance prep step of draining the yogurt for about 8 hours. It's easy to do and creates a much smoother, silkier frozen yogurt. Put a sieve over a bowl and place two layers of cheesecloth over the sieve. Plop a whole quart of low-fat yogurt on top and let it sit in your refrigerator for about 8 hours.

COOK Pour the milk, cream, sugar, and corn syrup into a saucepan. Bring to a boil and set a timer for precisely 4 minutes—the timing is critical. Turn off the heat and whisk in the cornstarch slurry. Return to a boil to slightly thicken.

CHILL Whisk the hot milk mixture into the cream cheese. Do this a little bit at a time so that you can whip out any lumps of cream cheese. Pour the hot ice cream base into a Ziploc bag and seal. Submerge in the ice bath until very cold.

FREEZE Cut the corner off the bag, pour the chilled base into the ice cream machine, and turn on the machine. When finished, transfer to a storage container and freeze until firm, about 4 hours.

HOW TO TELL WHEN YOUR ICE CREAM IS DONE **For Ice Creams** The ice cream is finished at the exact moment when the machine isn't freezing the ice cream anymore; the ice cream will begin to pull away from the sides (about 25 minutes). **For Sorbets** Sorbets are done when they achieve the consistency of a thick smoothie; they should be frozen enough to be just barely pourable. If you fully freeze sorbets, too much air will be whipped in and they will become fluffy and crumbly.

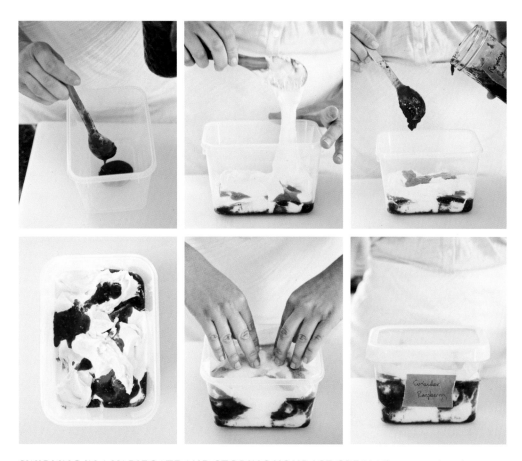

SWIRLING IN A VARIEGATE AND STORING YOUR ICE CREAM If you are packing the ice cream with a sauce (or variegate), alternate layers, creating pockets with the sauce. Be sure to put a bit on the bottom of the container and reserve some to put on the top of the ice cream. If you are adding chunks, layer them in evenly as you go.

Then, working quickly, pack the ice cream into a container, cover with parchment paper or wax paper to seal out air, and let the flavors bloom while it hardens in your freezer for at least 4 hours.

SERVE When you remove the ice cream from the freezer, let it sit and relax for 5 to 10 minutes before you scoop and serve it—it doesn't need to melt, but it does need to thaw slightly. Ideally, serve and eat it while it's quite firm but pliable and you are able to easily roll it into a ball. Once you've scooped it, return any remaining ice cream to the freezer. If the ice cream has melted too much at room temperature, refreezing it will result in an ice cream that is too icy.

INGREDIENTS & EQUIPMENT

Ice cream making requires attention to the smallest details—the type of milk you use, even the kind of saucepan you choose. Certain variables can throw off the texture and flavor of anything you make. That said, for the most part, the recipes here are easy, and in no time, you will be creating artisan ice creams at home!

• • • • ●

Ingredients

DAIRY PRODUCTS Use whole milk and heavy cream. If you have access to nonhomogenized, grass-pastured milk, you will be able to achieve the best flavor, but you will have to take the extra step to homogenize the mixture (see page 193).

When yogurt is called for, we use **low-fat plain yogurt,** which is strained to get rid of excess liquid. This method produces creamier frozen yogurt than using thicker Greek-style yogurt.

I prefer Organic Valley **cream cheese,** because it is a true cultured cheese and has a clean dairy flavor and minimal natural thickeners, but any full-fat cream cheese will work.

CHOCOLATE The better the quality, the more complex the flavor. You can choose whatever chocolate you like when making chocolate flecks for ice cream, but when it comes to chocolate ice cream, use a chocolate that has at least 60% cacao. We tend to go much higher when we make chocolate ice cream at Jeni's, even when making milk chocolate, because adding milk and cream softens the flavor of any chocolate considerably. We love Askinosie Chocolate, but we live in a world full of superb chocolates: Valrhona, Green & Black's,

Ghirardelli, El Rey, and Callebaut all are great options.

EXTRACTS & FLAVORINGS Extracts and flavorings are invaluable in ice cream making because they are potent in very small amounts and therefore adding them won't affect the texture of the ice cream. We almost always use pure natural flavorings, which are made by steeping herbs or spices in a carrier like alcohol or oil. We often go straight to the source and use undiluted essential oils, which are volatile, concentrated scents from certain parts of plants, such as citrus zest, basil leaves, cinnamon bark, or coriander seeds. Vanilla extract is the most common in our kitchen; we use an extract produced right on a farm in Uganda. We also seem to find infinite uses for the natural butter flavor from Frontier Natural Products (it is actually made from butter solids; see Sources, page 208). I steer clear of artificial flavorings unless there is a compelling reason for one—as in the nostalgic push-ups made with Kool-Aid (see page 83).

CORN SYRUP & TAPIOCA SYRUP Both these syrups are sugars composed primarily of glucose, which has a moisture-attracting quality

that sucrose (granulated sugar) does not have. These syrups are natural and very useful tools in ice cream making. Less sweet than table sugar, glucose helps prevent ice crystals and gives a bit of elasticity to the ice cream. We use tapioca syrup in our kitchen, in addition to regular sugar, but I call for corn syrup in these recipes because it is easier to find. Either one will work, but avoid high-fructose corn syrup—it's too sweet for these recipes. (Tapioca syrup is available at natural foods markets.)

CORNSTARCH & TAPIOCA STARCH

These natural thickeners absorb and hold water, so that it does not crystallize in the frozen ice cream. We use tapioca starch in our ice creams because it works better with the way we cook our cream, but I call for cornstarch in these recipes because cornstarch is more readily available. You can use whichever you like. (See Sources, page 208.)

Equipment

All of these ice creams can be made with ordinary home equipment. The only special item you will need is an ice cream machine. Here is a list of the equipment that we used daily when testing these home ice cream recipes.

ICE CREAM MACHINE I developed these recipes using a Cuisinart Ice-20 1½-quart canister machine. You can use any similar machine.

An electric canister machine has a motor housed in the base and a canister filled with a coolant that must first be frozen for 24 hours. The plastic dasher (blade) is fitted into the canister, the top covers the entire thing, and when the machine is turned on, the canister spins the top and keeps the dasher immobile. The dasher scrapes the sides of the spinning canister as ice crystals form, moving the small crystals to the middle of the canister, where they are tumbled with other crystals and smoothed out. A small amount of air is incorporated. When the ice cream is done, it will begin to pull away from the sides. The ice cream will still be soft, but the ice crystal structure is intact and stable. Finish the freezing by transferring the ice cream to a storage container and hardening it in the freezer.

Important: The first time you use the machine, you need to freeze the canister for a full 24 hours. If the canister is not cold enough, your ice cream won't freeze. Then, each time you make ice cream, immediately wash the canister, dry it, and stick it back into the freezer; if it warms to room temperature, it needs another full 24 hours to refreeze.

If you want to make more than one flavor on any one day, you will need an extra canister or two; many machines now come with two. Because the recipes in this book produce ice creams that keep in a very cold freezer for up to a week (or more), you could make one ice cream per day for several days, using the same canister, and have a wide selection for a party.

Although more expensive, self-contained freezing models exist, I discovered that I actually prefer the less-expensive canister type. It freezes the ice cream faster. The housings of the self-contained freezing models heat up after the first batch of ice cream, and when you are making more than one ice cream, it takes longer and longer with each successive batch to freeze the ice cream.

4-QUART HEAVY-BOTTOMED SAUCEPAN If you have just a 3-quart saucepan, you can use it for my recipes, but watch it carefully so that the milk doesn't boil over.

FOOD PROCESSOR We use one for chopping or pulverizing nuts and fruits and for making purees and sauces.

BAKING DISHES AND PANS We use 9-inch square glass or ceramic baking dishes for cakes and roasting fruits. A professional quarter sheet pan is a bit harder to locate, but it's handy for making marshmallows and pralines. A half-sheet pan will work and is also very useful for meringues and brittles.

THREE BOWLS I prefer metal bowls, which can be used for mixing as well as for improvising a double boiler. For most of these recipes, you'll need large, medium, and small sizes.

WHISK A good-quality medium stainless steel whisk is essential for incorporating the cream cheese into the cream. I also prefer it for whipping cream.

MEASURING CUPS, MEASURING SPOONS
Liquid measuring cups have pouring spouts and are made to hold liquids with room left over, to prevent spilling. Dry measuring cups are essentially scoops, and the ingredients they hold can be leveled across the top for accurate measuring. When making these recipes, always level your dry ingredients.

HEATPROOF SPATULA
Silicone spatulas are useful for stirring the ice cream base and other hot liquids. Find one that is one continuous piece; wooden-handled ones can harbor bacteria and be hard to clean.

SIEVE & CHEESECLOTH
A fine-mesh sieve and layers of cheesecloth are good for removing spices, teas, and coffee beans from the ice cream base and for draining liquid from yogurt.

HEAVY-DUTY 1-GALLON ZIPLOC FREEZER BAGS
The most efficient way to cool the hot ice cream base is to pour it into a plastic bag and submerge it in an ice water bath. Plastic bags offer the largest surface area, which cools the cream the fastest. And because they lie flat, they are a handy way to store the bases in the refrigerator if you are making many flavors.

PARCHMENT PAPER
We use parchment for covering the surface of the ice creams after packing them into storage containers and for baking. You can use wax paper for covering ice cream, but don't use plastic wrap since it can freeze into the folds of the ice cream.

ICE CREAM SCOOPER
Nothing beats a Zeroll scoop. The handle is filled with a liquid that transfers heat from your hand to the aluminum scoop, which cleanly releases the ice cream from the metal. We use them in our shops. In my experience, a disher, the scoop with a lever and spring, doesn't work well for ice cream.

FREEZER
It should be at or below 0°F to freeze the canister and store the ice cream. Use a freezer thermometer to check the temperature.

THE CRAFT OF ICE CREAM

I learned very early on that my artistic leanings could take me only so far in making great ice creams. All those years I'd spent avoiding science classes in high school and college came back to haunt me when I started working with frozen confectionery. Freezing ice cream into a smooth, lickable, delicious mass is a very precise process. Math and science are required.

● ● ● ● ●

In recent years, I've had a lot of fun going around to schools and talking to kids about the importance of these subjects. An aspiring artist growing up, I couldn't imagine when I would ever use more than basic math. My teachers never explained the importance of math and science in a way that satisfied me. When I go out and speak to kids, I am very clear: Science is everything—even to artists. And creativity is everything—even to scientists. But you can follow the recipes and make splendid ice cream without reading another word of this chapter. Or you can roll up your sleeves and learn the basic science behind the art.

Ice cream is a frozen emulsion of water, butterfat (the concentrated fat in milk), proteins (whey and casein), sugars (sucrose, glucose, lactose, and others), starch (thickener), air, and flavors. The balance of all these ingredients, on a molecular level, determines the flavor, texture, consistency, and finish of the ice cream. Other additions (fruit, chocolate, alcohol, etc.) can disrupt the balance. In addition, if the proportions of water, protein, and fat are out of balance, it can make the ice cream feel too cold or too warm on the palate. Understanding the interplay of these ingredients on a molecular level is what ice cream making is all about. The recipes in

this book are relatively foolproof for an average cook, but when you branch off on your own, the scientific overview that follows might help you craft your newest flavor.

BALANCING INGREDIENTS

If you were staring out the window during high school chemistry, don't worry—this won't hurt a bit. If any component is not in balance with the water, the ice cream will be "short" (crumbly), soggy, or icy. The perfect balance of ingredients also allows the right amount of air—not too much or too little—to be whipped into the ice cream.

WATER Water is either with you or against you when it comes to making ice creams. It's with you when you have perfectly balanced ingredients that cause water molecules to bind with the proteins, starches, sugars, and fats. It's against you when it roams "unbound" in the mix, leaving you with icy or soggy homemade ice cream.

We don't think of water when we think of ice cream, right? We think of milk. Well, milk is almost 90 percent water. Water will bind to fats, proteins, sugars, and starches—but reluctantly. Free unbound water will become coarse, crunchy ice crystals. Any liquid you add to your ice cream contains water, from milk and honey to berry purees and beer. The goal is to bind the water to sugar, protein, fat, or starch, which will help prevent it from turning into ice crystals. Although each component will bind some water, no single ingredient will take care of all the water so we use a perfect balance of ingredients. Other than pleasing yourself and all who will eat your splendid ice cream, you have one ultimate goal: to bind those water molecules in the milk.

BUTTERFAT Butterfat is the fat in milk. When you remove nonfat skim milk from whole milk, you get heavy cream. If you agitate heavy cream for a while, the fat will separate from the watery, protein-rich whey and you will have butter. Butter is 87 percent butterfat, and butterfat is what makes the ice cream rich and lush. In addition to providing creaminess to the ice cream, butterfat is a great carrier of flavor. It is known to absorb flavors readily—if you store butter next to an onion, the butter will begin to smell like onions. Making ice cream is essentially harnessing flavor. By flavoring butterfat with all things tasty, you lock flavor into your ice cream—which will then be released by the warmth of your tongue and explode into your nose. Unlike egg yolk fat and some other fats, butterfat melts at body temperature. (It releases flavor and scent as soon as it hits your palate.) Lower-butterfat ice creams don't linger as long on your palate or in your nose.

Too much butterfat, and the ice cream will be cloying, and, well, too buttery. Too little, and the ice cream will be thin and weak-bodied and have a mysterious lack of flavor. The flavor of butterfat itself is creamy and lush—a perfect complement to almost any other flavor.

PROTEIN Many ice cream recipes call for egg yolks, which thicken cream by binding water when heated (the protein binds water and coagulates into a custard). However, milk naturally contains the essential proteins necessary to bind water and fat and add body to the ice cream, and these proteins do a better job than egg proteins do.

The two main protein groups in milk are casein and whey. Heat and acid will "denature" the protein (forcing the protein to shed its protective outer coating), which makes it likely to bind with water and thicken the cream. Heating the milk evaporates some of the water, which concentrates the protein and makes the ice creams smoother.

A small lump of cream cheese, which is high in casein proteins (achieved by adding acid to the milk), helps bind the ingredients and gives the ice cream body.

SUGAR Different sugars have different binding capabilities. Sucrose (table sugar) is very sweet and will bind some water. Glucose (from corn or tapioca syrup) has the most water-binding capability and is much less sweet than sucrose. Adding a bit of corn syrup (or tapioca syrup) in place of table sugar actually makes the ice cream less sweet; too much will give the ice cream a soggy texture. Lactose is sugar naturally present in small amounts in milk; it provides some sweetness to the ice cream.

STARCH Cornstarch (or tapioca starch) is the insurance policy on your road to delicious ice creams and yogurts. Any water that dreams of roaming unbound and transforming into nasty, long ice crystals has no choice but to bind with the cornstarch. It is especially important when you add more water-packed ingredients to ice cream or yogurt.

AIR An ice cream's creaminess is in part determined by its air content. All ice cream contains some amount of air. Too much, and the ice cream is too fluffy. Too little, and it becomes a dense, unscoopable mass.

SENSORY COMPONENTS OF ICE CREAMS

TASTE I draw on all the taste sensations experienced on your tongue—sweet, sour, bitter, salty, savory, piquant (chile peppers), and cool (mint, menthol). Taste is the first tier of the four-layered ice cream experience.

TEXTURE It's that crunch between your teeth, that fine-grained grit between your tongue and the roof of your mouth. It's the way viscous, protein-rich butterfat feels inside your mouth. The texture of my ice cream? As smooth and as creamy as I can possibly make it or as chunky, bumpy, and full of nuts, fruits, or handmade goodies as it can be.

CONSISTENCY Consistency refers to the "body" of the ice cream: heavy or light, chewy or weak and thin, hard- or soft-frozen. I strive for body that is dense without being heavy or cloying and just a bit chewy, with a clean, thin "meltdown." We serve our ice cream in a hard-frozen state so that you can eat it slowly from a cone and savor it without it melting quickly.

FINISH You've swallowed the smooth, creamy ice cream, but the pleasant aroma lingers in your nose—that's the "finish," the flavor the butterfat releases as it melts on your tongue and blooms into your nose.

TAKING OFF ON YOUR OWN: CRAFTING ICE CREAMS

Almost anything you add to ice cream will upset the balance of ingredients. When experimenting with flavors, begin by adding a minimal amount of any ingredient to gradually increase flavor with minimal impact on texture. Keep notes so you can adjust each batch and learn how ingredients affect the finished product.

Most flavors are either oil soluble or water soluble. The scents of cinnamon, coffee, mint, basil, and others are essential oils naturally present in plant matter; they bind easily with butterfat because they are oil soluble. (They will also bind with high-proof alcohol, which is how extracts are made.) Fresh fruits and citrus juices hold all of their flavor in the water of the flesh and will not bind with the cream. They are water-soluble essences and must be used sparingly to avoid iciness.

OIL-SOLUBLE AROMATICS To release oil-soluble aromatics into the ice cream base, use a cold or hot steep. We employ both techniques daily in our production kitchen. Hard, dried, barky ingredients require heat. For instance, for coffee ice cream, we add coffee to hot cream and allow it to steep for 10 minutes; we then pour the hot, flavored cream through a sieve to remove the grounds. Green herbs are more delicate and do better with a cold steep. When we make fresh mint ice cream, the mint is torn and muddled, then added to cold cream. It will infuse for about 12 hours and then be removed.

WATER-SOLUBLE FLAVORS For water-soluble ingredients—such as melons, berries, cucumbers, or stone fruits—puree the flesh and add it directly to the ice cream. Berries and melons hold all of their scents in the watery pulp of the fruit, which doesn't bond with alcohol or fats. There is no way to fully separate the flavor from the water; therefore, to keep your ice creams from becoming too icy, it's usually best to concentrate the flavors by heating and evaporating some of the water—as in the roasting strawberries technique (see page 31), which can be applied to most stone fruits and berries. You can also pulverize the fruit and heat the puree with just enough sugar to bind the water to the sugar (about 1 part sugar to 3 parts fruit). Be sure to warm rather than cook the fruit; you don't want the fruit to become "jammy."

EXTRACTS & ESSENTIAL OILS Extracts are made by steeping plant matter in alcohol or oil, which, like butterfat, will bond with the flavorful essential oils of plants. Most flavor extracts are made from oil-soluble scents such as vanilla, cinnamon, and almond. Extracts should be used just before freezing, so that the flavor is not evaporated in the heating process. How much you will need depends on how concentrated the extract is (1/2 to 2 teaspoons is a good range).

Essential oils are pressed or distilled directly from plant matter. An essential oil is the "essence" of a plant and it is highly concentrated; 2 to 5 drops are enough to flavor a whole batch. Add essential oils drop by drop to the ice cream just after you turn the machine on to spin.

SOFT CHEESES & NUT BUTTERS Add these to the warm cream mixture as it comes off the stove. Add them a little at a time, incorporating each addition completely before adding more.

HARD CHEESES Steep hard cheeses as you would mint or other ingredients, and then strain them. Finely grate the cheese and, if you can, add the hard rind to the boiling step (especially with Parmesan). Allow it all to sit in the cream until the cream is cold, then strain and remove any unincorporated cheese.

ALCOHOL Alcohol will depress the freezing point of ice cream, so it will take longer to freeze and/or stay softer, but sometimes this can be deceiving. Stout, for example, has very low alcohol content; you can add it in small quantities without reducing the sugar or adding more. For spirits with very high alcohol—say, bourbon—1/4 cup or less can be added to the basic recipe with no problem. If you wish to add more than that, you should reduce the sugar by a few tablespoons. Add the alcohol to the chilled ice cream base just before freezing.

SUGARS It's important to keep the sugar ratio the same in the recipe, or your ice cream will become too hard or too soupy. If you want to add honey, you will need to remove an equal portion of table sugar from the recipe (again, to keep the sugar ratio in balance). Never substitute honey for more than 25 percent of the total sugar, or the ice cream will be too sweet and icy. If you want to add maple syrup, reduce it on the stove by one third and use it in place of a portion of the sugar in the recipe (see page 114). Brown sugar, turbinado, and cane sugar can all be used interchangeably.

COCOA POWDER & CHOCOLATES Adding chocolate to the ice cream base can make ice cream crumbly or dry. It's best to start with one of the recipes in this book, such as The Milkiest Chocolate Ice Cream in the World (page 156) or The Darkest Chocolate Ice Cream in the World (page 100), and go from there. Hydrated cocoa will give you the strongest flavor.

I alternate between using Dutch-process and nonalkalized cocoa. Dutch-process cocoa yields balanced and more nuanced chocolate flavor and has a rich color. Nonalkalized cocoa, which is lighter in color, yields a sharper, fruitier flavor—a nice contrast to the fullness of the cream. Melted chocolate isn't strong enough on its own. I like to add hard chocolate in its purest form by melting it and drizzling it into the finished ice cream (see page 104), especially if I am using a chocolate with unique characteristics that I want to shine through.

LEMON
BLUEBERR
YOGUR

spring

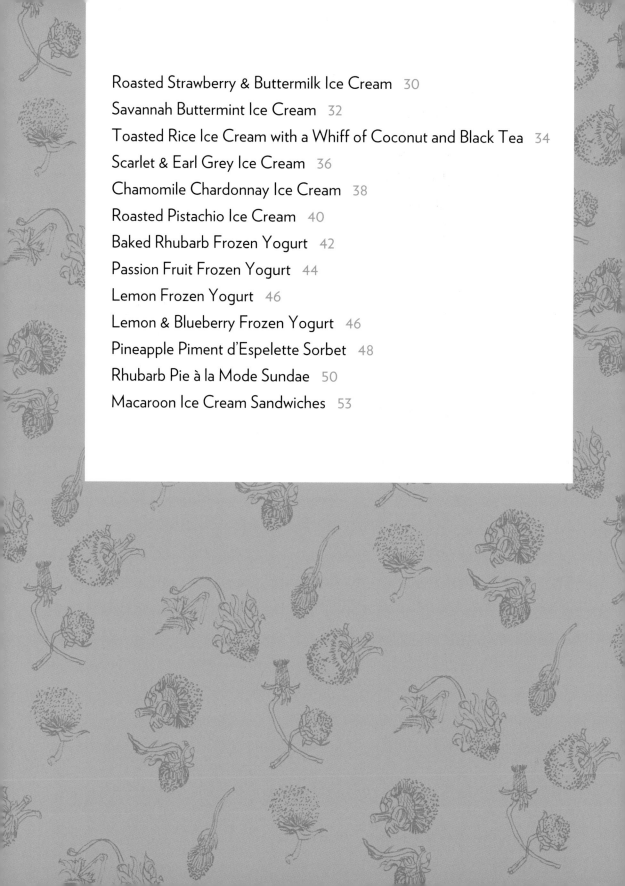

GLORIOUS SPRING. At first it's really more of a promise, and yet we welcome it and impatiently fling off our winter coats too early in anticipation. Those rainy, windy days of March and April that only reluctantly give way to rhubarb, strawberries, ramps, and morels offer little solace after the cold, snowy days of winter, but it's enough. It's hope and new beginnings, new life and the comfort of knowing that spring has come again.

Our kitchen boosts its production in the early days of April. Although our customers have shown us that every season is ice cream season, spring and summer remain the busiest ones for us. After a dreary winter, our customers are craving color in their lives and the lively flavors of fresh fruit. They can hardly wait for the first batch of Lemon & Blueberry Frozen Yogurt or Roasted Strawberry & Buttermilk Ice Cream. In spring, Farmer Lee Jones of The Chefs' Garden sometimes surprises us with a box of treats: pineapple mint and other lemony things that he grows in greenhouses. These first scarce signs of the abundant warm days to come satisfy our desire for lightness and flavor after a long winter.

Our entire company transforms with each season, and in the spring, the kitchen shifts from baking and candy making to chopping and pureeing fruits as they make their way from garden to kitchen to ice cream. The pounding sound of breaking up almond brittle ceases, and we enjoy the new silence of our days spent all-hands-on-deck at the enormous table, cutting rhubarb or strawberries. When the local strawberries are in season, our small team will wash, hull, puree, and freeze more than eight thousand pounds of those tiny red jewels in one week. After three weeks, they are gone from the fields of Ohio, and we hope that we have enough to get us to September.

The scent of the kitchen and even the street out front transform from winter's brown butter and vanilla to the sprightly fragrance of thousands of berries. Our art department begins using vibrant colors in preparation for the early harvest campaign. And our shopkeepers remove their winter décor, open the doors for the season, and begin serving our new seasonal ice creams and sundaes to eager customers. New employees are trained in the craft of gracious service, and managers get ready for the onslaught of long lines out the doors from April through September.

WARREN & SNOWVILLE

The quality of the cream is what truly sets American artisan ice cream apart from the other ice creams in the grocery aisle. Flavor blooms when built on an exquisite foundation.

• • • • •

There are two things I need as an ice cream maker: (1) the ability to tweak ingredients during every step of the ice-cream-making process (which required years of practice and learning the science) and (2) a partnership with a great dairy.

Meet Warren Taylor, the Don Quixote of dairymen! When they write the history of the deconstruction of our industrialized food system, Warren Taylor will be in paragraph one. Passionately devoted to making good, fresh, and nutritious dairy products safe and widely available without the use of industrial-farming techniques, Warren, who is in his early sixties, has more energy than anyone I have ever met. He never stops talking—about everything. He is the only person I know who can seamlessly weave Beat poetry, biblical references, Confucian philosophy, and Jefferson Airplane lyrics into a conversation about retooling Ohio and America's dairy industry.

At Snowville Creamery, a small-scale dairy in southeast Ohio, Warren works with neighbors Bill Dix and Stacy Hall to process milk from cows that graze on grass.

Good milk, what Warren calls "milk the way it used to be," has always been one of the most important things in life to him. Warren, who built his humble dairy with his retirement, his life savings, spent his career as a dairy scientist watching milk quality diminish. Every region of America deserves a Warren Taylor—someone who is "all in" when it comes to cultivating great minimally processed milk and cream.

Warren and his Snowville crew milk Bill and Stacy's cows twice a day and deliver their high-butterfat (16 percent) cream to us within thirty-six hours of milking. We buy almost all of Warren's high-butterfat cream to make our ice creams. Our do-it-yourself companies are growing and working together each step of the way, and our partnership is proof that a new, more robust food system can work.

Artisan ice cream must start with Snowville's kind of minimally processed milk and cream, which are more healthful and flavorful than conventional overly processed, overly pasteurized milk and cream. Milk and cream produced by cows that eat grass contain the sweet smell and taste (and nutritional benefits) of grass. How fortunate we are for that.

ROASTED STRAWBERRY & BUTTERMILK ICE CREAM

A bright and pure strawberry ice cream. Buttermilk draws out the true flavor of fresh strawberries.

When Ohio strawberries are at their peak, we buy up thousands of pounds per week from neighboring farms. We quickly wash, hull, and freeze them—so we can make strawberry ice cream all summer long.

The best strawberries are juicy, fragrant, and sweet but have a tart edge. Roasting them for just a few minutes evaporates some of the water and concentrates the flavor. A touch of lemon juice and buttermilk helps draw out the subtle tartness of the berries.

We never put pieces of strawberries in ice cream; because of their high water content, they freeze into rock-hard, flavorless chunks. Instead, we puree the berries to flavor the ice cream. You will have extra roasted strawberry puree (it's necessary to fill the baking dish with berries so they don't scorch or dry out too much as they roast), but you can serve it over other ice creams.

Pairs well with: Reduction of balsamic vinegar. Almond cake. Roasted Pistachio Ice Cream (page 40). Rose water.

Makes about 1 quart

ROASTED STRAWBERRIES
1 pint strawberries, hulled and sliced ½ inch thick

⅓ cup sugar

3 tablespoons fresh lemon juice

ICE CREAM BASE
1½ cups whole milk

2 tablespoons cornstarch

2 ounces (4 tablespoons) cream cheese, softened

⅛ teaspoon fine sea salt

1¼ cups heavy cream

⅔ cup sugar

2 tablespoons light corn syrup

¼ cup buttermilk

TASTING NOTES

_____

_____

_____

_____

_____

PREP

For the strawberries:

Preheat the oven to 375°F. Combine the strawberries with the sugar in an 8-inch square glass or ceramic baking dish, stirring gently to mix well. Roast for 8 minutes, or until just soft. Let cool slightly.

Puree the berries in a food processor with the lemon juice. Measure 1/2 cup of the pureed berries; refrigerate the rest of the puree for another use.

For the ice cream base:

Mix about 2 tablespoons of the milk with the cornstarch in a small bowl to make a smooth slurry. Whisk the cream cheese and salt in a medium bowl until smooth. Fill a large bowl with ice and water.

COOK Combine the remaining milk, the cream, sugar, and corn syrup in a 4-quart saucepan, bring to a rolling boil over medium-high heat, and boil for 4 minutes. Remove from the heat and gradually whisk in the cornstarch slurry. Bring the mixture to a boil over medium-high heat and cook, stirring with a heatproof spatula, until slightly thickened, about 1 minute. Remove from the heat.

CHILL Gradually whisk the hot milk mixture into the cream cheese until smooth. Add the reserved 1/2 cup strawberry puree and the buttermilk and blend well. Pour the mixture into a 1-gallon Ziploc freezer bag and submerge the sealed bag in the ice bath. Let stand, adding more ice as necessary, until cold, about 30 minutes.

FREEZE Pour the ice cream base into the frozen canister and spin until thick and creamy.

Pack the ice cream into a storage container, press a sheet of parchment directly against the surface, and seal with an airtight lid. Freeze in the coldest part of your freezer until firm, at least 4 hours.

SAVANNAH BUTTERMINT ICE CREAM

A salty, buttery mint ice cream with white chocolate flecks. Turmeric adds a soft ivory yellow.

Savannah Buttermint Ice Cream was inspired by the pastel-colored white chocolate disks found in old-timey chocolate shops and those powdery, melt-in-your-mouth mint candies in the restaurants of our grandparents' generation. It's slightly salty, minty, and very buttery. The white chocolate flecks give it a pronounced creaminess.

There is a special ingredient in this ice cream: the butter flavor. It's one of very few flavorings that we stock in our kitchen, but believe me, it's the right thing here. We use one from Frontier Natural Products, and it's potently concentrated. A bit of turmeric gives the ice cream color but no added flavor. The creamy pale yellow hue sets the mood for buttermint: Easter baskets, white gloves, and baby showers.

Pairs well with: Wedding cake. Chocolate cake or fudge brownies. Milk chocolate bunnies.

Makes about 1 quart

2 cups whole milk

1 tablespoon plus 1 teaspoon cornstarch

1½ ounces (3 tablespoons) cream cheese, softened

½ teaspoon fine sea salt

⅛ teaspoon turmeric

1¼ cups heavy cream

⅔ cup sugar

2 tablespoons light corn syrup

3 ounces white chocolate, chopped

8 drops natural butter flavor (see Sources, page 208)

3 to 4 drops pure peppermint essential oil (see Sources, page 208)

TASTING NOTES

_____

_____

_____

_____

_____

_____

PREP Mix about 2 tablespoons of the milk with the cornstarch in a small bowl to make a smooth slurry.

Whisk the cream cheese, salt, and turmeric in a medium bowl until smooth. Fill a large bowl with ice and water.

COOK Combine the remaining milk, the cream, sugar, and corn syrup in a 4-quart saucepan, bring to a rolling boil over medium-high heat, and boil for 4 minutes. Remove from the heat and gradually whisk in the cornstarch slurry. Bring the mixture back to a boil over medium-high heat and cook, stirring with a heatproof spatula, until slightly thickened, about 1 minute. Remove from the heat.

CHILL Gradually whisk the hot milk mixture into the cream cheese until smooth. Pour the mixture into a 1-gallon Ziploc freezer bag, and submerge the sealed bag in the ice bath. Let stand, adding more ice as necessary, until cold, about 30 minutes.

FREEZE When the ice cream is almost ready to be churned, melt the white chocolate in a double boiler; let cool slightly.

Pour the ice cream base into the frozen canister and turn on the machine. Drop the butter flavoring and peppermint through the opening in the top of the machine. Slowly drizzle in the melted chocolate; it will form into flecks in the churning cream. Continue to spin the ice cream until thick and creamy.

Pack the ice cream into a storage container, press a sheet of parchment directly against the surface, and seal with an airtight lid. Freeze in the coldest part of your freezer until firm, at least 4 hours.

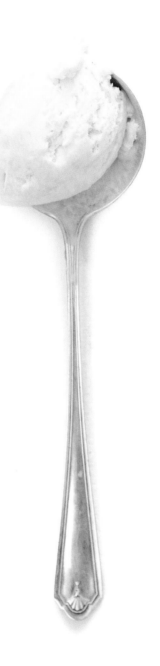

SCARLET & EARL GREY ICE CREAM

Bergamot-scented black tea and sugar-plumped cherries: sweet and civilized.

Although tannins, the chemical compounds that create that "gripping" feeling in the mouth, are typically associated with red wine, tea leaves also contain large amounts.

Earl Grey tea is flavored with oil of bergamot, which is cold-pressed from the rind of a small orange grown mainly in the Calabria region of Italy. It is a sour citrus fruit with bitter notes prized for the fragrance of its zest. The scent of bergamot is unlike that of any other citrus fruit. It is astringent, piney, and bitter orange.

Pairs well with: Chocolate. Cookies. Cannoli with ricotta and chocolate chips.

Makes about 1 quart

2 cups whole milk

1 tablespoon plus 1 teaspoon cornstarch

1½ ounces (3 tablespoons) cream cheese, softened

1¼ cups heavy cream

⅔ cup sugar

2 tablespoons light corn syrup

¼ cup Earl Grey tea leaves

2 cups Sugar-Plumped Cherries (page 194)

TASTING NOTES

_____

_____

_____

_____

_____

_____

PREP Mix about 2 tablespoons of the milk with the cornstarch in a small bowl to make a smooth slurry.

Whisk the cream cheese in a medium bowl until smooth.

Fill a large bowl with ice and water.

COOK Combine the remaining milk, the cream, sugar, and corn syrup in a 4-quart saucepan, bring to a rolling boil over medium-high heat, and boil for 4 minutes. Remove from the heat, add the tea, and let steep for 10 minutes.

Strain the milk mixture through a fine sieve, pressing on the tea leaves to extract as much cream as possible. Return to the saucepan and gradually whisk in the cornstarch slurry. Bring back to a boil over medium-high heat and cook, stirring with a heatproof spatula, until slightly thickened, about 1 minute. Remove from the heat.

CHILL Gradually whisk the hot milk mixture into the cream cheese until smooth.

Pour the mixture into a 1-gallon Ziploc freezer bag and submerge the sealed bag in the ice bath. Let stand, adding more ice as necessary, until cold, about 30 minutes.

FREEZE Pour the ice cream base into the frozen canister and spin until thick and creamy. Drain the cherries well.

Pack the ice cream into a storage container, layering it with the cherries as you go. Press a sheet of parchment directly against the surface and seal with an airtight lid. Freeze in the coldest part of your freezer until firm, at least 4 hours.

ROASTED PISTACHIO ICE CREAM

Pure, true pistachio flavor with a salted-nut finish.

The bright green pistachios from Sicily and Iran are gorgeous (and expensive), but when it comes to flavor, I prefer the California variety. My favorite pistachios in the shell are from Sunkist. Our pistachio ice cream is a warm, mossy green, and it doesn't hit you with a powerful fake nut flavor as many pistachio-flavored desserts do. Instead, it begins with subtlety, the rich nuttiness growing with each bite. This is a highly satisfying ice cream with nearly savory qualities.

Pairs well with: Strawberries. Basil. Mango frozen yogurt.

Makes about 1 quart

½ cup shelled unsalted pistachios (plus ¼ to ½ cup if you want to add whole ones to your ice cream)

2 cups whole milk

1 tablespoons plus 1 teaspoon cornstarch

1½ ounces (3 tablespoons) cream cheese, softened

½ teaspoon fine sea salt

1¼ cups heavy cream

⅔ cup sugar

2 tablespoons light corn syrup

½ teaspoon almond extract

TASTING NOTES

_____

_____

_____

_____

_____

PREP Preheat the oven to 350°F.

Spread the ½ cup pistachios out on a small baking sheet and toast in the oven for 10 to 12 minutes, until fragrant and just starting to brown. Remove from the oven and pulverize in a food processor until the pistachios become a very smooth paste.

Mix about 2 tablespoons of the milk with the cornstarch in a small bowl to make a smooth slurry.

Whisk the cream cheese, pistachio paste, and salt in a medium bowl until smooth.

Fill a large bowl with ice and water.

COOK Combine the remaining milk, the cream, sugar, and corn syrup in a 4-quart saucepan, bring to a rolling boil over medium-high heat, and boil for 4 minutes. Remove from the heat and gradually whisk in the cornstarch slurry.

Bring the mixture back to a boil over medium-high heat and cook, stirring with a heatproof spatula, until slightly thickened, about 1 minute. Remove from the heat.

CHILL Gradually whisk the hot milk mixture into the cream cheese mixture until smooth.

Pour the mixture into a 1-gallon Ziploc freezer bag and submerge the sealed bag in the ice bath. Let stand, adding more ice as necessary, until cold, about 30 minutes.

FREEZE Pour the ice cream base into the frozen canister and turn on the machine. Pour the almond extract into the opening in the top of the machine and continue to spin the ice cream until thick and creamy.

Pack the ice cream into a storage container, layering it with the whole pistachios, if using, as you go. Press a sheet of parchment directly against the surface, and seal with an airtight lid. Freeze in the coldest part of your freezer until firm, at least 4 hours.

PASSION FRUIT FROZEN YOGURT

Intensely aromatic passion fruit, almost as tart as lemon, is complemented by cool yogurt and grounded by fresh cream.

To me, passion fruit is the flavor of travel. In so many places in the world, passion fruits fall off the trees. They are everywhere and everything, it seems, is flavored with them: soft drinks and cocktails, shaved ice, ice cream, cheesecake and other desserts, and candies. When I was younger, I went to Puerto Rico several times, and it was there that I fell in love with the intense flavor of fresh passion fruit. It's great for spring, when local fruits are not yet available but we are craving lighter flavors for the warmer days. Passion fruit is sunshine in a bite.

Passion fruit pulp is great for making frozen yogurt, because a little goes a long way, which means that the yogurt won't be icy from too much added water.

Pairs well with: Pastries with floral notes, such as lavender pound cake.
Dark chocolate. Young coconut.

Makes a generous 1 quart

FROZEN YOGURT BASE

1 quart plain low-fat yogurt

1½ cups whole milk

2 tablespoons cornstarch

2 ounces (4 tablespoons) cream cheese, softened

½ cup heavy cream

⅔ cup sugar

¼ cup light corn syrup

PASSION FRUIT SYRUP

6 large or 8 medium passion fruits

3 tablespoons sugar

TASTING NOTES

_____

_____

_____

_____

_____

_____

ADVANCE PREP

For the frozen yogurt base:
Fit a sieve over a bowl and line it with two layers of cheesecloth. Pour the yogurt into the sieve, cover with plastic wrap, and refrigerate for 6 to 8 hours to drain. Discard the liquid, and measure out 1¼ cups of the strained yogurt; set aside.

PREP

For the passion fruit syrup:
Set a sieve over a bowl. Slice each passion fruit in half and scoop the flesh of the fruit into the sieve. Using a spatula or wooden spoon, push the fruit through the sieve, leaving the seeds behind.

Measure out ½ cup of the passion fruit pulp and combine it with the sugar in a small saucepan. Bring to a boil over medium-high heat, stirring to dissolve the sugar. Remove from the heat and let cool.

For the frozen yogurt base:
Mix about 3 tablespoons of the milk with the cornstarch in a small bowl to make a smooth slurry.

Whisk the cream cheese in a medium bowl until smooth.

Fill a large bowl with ice and water.

COOK Combine the remaining milk, the cream, sugar, and corn syrup in a 4-quart saucepan, bring to a rolling boil over medium-high heat, and boil for 4 minutes. Remove from the heat and gradually whisk in the cornstarch mixture.

Bring the mixture back to a boil over medium-high heat and cook, stirring with a heatproof spatula, until slightly thickened, about 1 minute. Remove from the heat.

CHILL Gradually whisk the hot milk mixture into the cream cheese until smooth. Add the reserved 1¼ cups drained yogurt and the passion fruit syrup and whisk until smooth.

Pour the mixture into a 1-gallon Ziploc freezer bag and submerge the sealed bag in the ice bath. Let stand, adding more ice as necessary, until cold, about 30 minutes.

FREEZE Pour the yogurt base into the frozen canister and spin until thick and creamy.

Pack the frozen yogurt into a storage container, press a sheet of parchment directly against the surface, and seal with an airtight lid. Freeze in the coldest part of your freezer until firm, at least 4 hours.

PINEAPPLE PIMENT D'ESPELETTE SORBET

Pulverized fresh pineapple with a surprising punch of sweet, mild pepper.

Piment d'Espelette is a small pepper grown in the Basque region of southern France. When it's dried and crushed, its sweet, smoky flavor is similar to that of paprika, with peppery undernotes that add a dash of round heat. Piment d'Espelette is becoming more widely available in specialty grocery stores, and it can be ordered online (see Sources, page 208). You can also leave the piment out of the sorbet itself and sprinkle it generously on top instead.

Pairs well with: Carrot cake. Salty Caramel Ice Cream (page 102). Mascarpone. Whipped cream.

Makes a generous 1 quart

1 pineapple (about 1½ pounds)

¾ cup sugar

⅓ cup corn syrup

3 tablespoons water

1 tablespoon piment d'Espelette or a scant 2 teaspoons sweet paprika plus a pinch of cayenne pepper

TASTING NOTES

_____

_____

_____

_____

_____

_____

PREP Using a large knife, cut off the base and top of the pineapple. Stand it upright on a cutting board and cut off the skin by slicing from top to bottom, turning the pineapple as you work. With the fruit still on end, slice the pineapple into quarters. Slice the tough core from each piece and cut the pineapple into large chunks. Puree in a food processor until smooth. Measure out 3 cups of the puree and set aside.

COOK Combine the sugar, corn syrup, water, and piment d'Espelette in a small saucepan and bring to a boil, stirring until the sugar is dissolved. Transfer to a medium bowl and let cool.

CHILL Combine the reserved pineapple puree with the sugar syrup. Chill thoroughly.

FREEZE Pour the sorbet base into the frozen canister and spin just until it is the consistency of very softly whipped cream.

   Pack the sorbet into a storage container, press a sheet of parchment directly against the surface, and seal with an airtight lid. Freeze in the coldest part of your freezer until firm, at least 4 hours.

a couple of spoonfuls
of Rhubarb Compote

a lot of
whipped
cream

1 Pie Crust Cookie

RHUBARB PIE À LA MODE SUNDAE

All the components of a great pie are there, but with elegant ease. You don't have to make a whole rhubarb pie—just roll out some pie crust, sprinkle with sugar, and bake in rounds to serve as a buttery, flaky garnish. Tart and aromatic Lime Cardamom Frozen Yogurt is a really great complement to rhubarb.

Pie à la Mode sundaes are in the interchangeable spirit of this book: serve any fruit sauce and ice cream with the pie crust "cookies" and whipped cream.

large scoop of Lime Cardamom Frozen Yogurt

Preheat the oven to 350°F. To make the Pie Crust Cookies, follow the directions for the Pie Crust on page 188 until you have rolled out the dough into a 1/4-inch-thick circle. Then chill for at least 30 minutes and up to 12 hours. Roll the dough out to 1/8 inch thick. Using a round 2- or 3-inch cookie cutter, cut 12 circles from the dough. Place the rounds on a parchment-lined baking sheet and, using a pastry brush, glaze each one lightly with some of the heavy cream. Sprinkle with some of the turbinado sugar. Bake in the oven until golden brown, 13 to 15 minutes. Let cool on a cooling rack. (You will need 6 Pie Crust Cookies for this recipe; the remaining cookies can be stored in an airtight container at room temperature for up to 3 days; if frozen, they keep for up to 2 weeks.)

To assemble the sundaes, place a pie crust cookie on a chilled plate or in a bowl. Top with a scoop of Lime Cardamom Frozen Yogurt and spoon over about 1/4 cup Rhubarb Compote. Finish with a generous dollop of Whipped Cream and, if desired, garnish with a lime twist.

Makes 6 servings

PIE CRUST COOKIES
Pie Crust (page 188)
1/4 cup heavy cream
2 tablespoons turbinado sugar

Lime Cardamom Frozen Yogurt (page 128)
Rhubarb Compote (see page 43)
Whipped Cream (page 203)
6 lime twists, for garnish (optional)

MACAROON ICE CREAM SANDWICHES

These cookies were inspired by Parisian *macarons*, but the recipe is not quite as fussy, and they work great for ice cream sandwiches. We make thousands of these a week in our kitchens and for many years they sold almost faster than we could make them. Thankfully, we've hired more people to help with production. The beauty of these colorful ice cream sandwiches is that the meringues are still soft and chewy, not frozen hard, when you bite into them.

These macaroons are normally made with almonds, but we also make them with pistachios and hazelnuts, as well as smoked almonds. If you go by weight, it's easy to switch nuts; I've also given the volume measures for other nuts.

Makes 6 sandwiches

MACAROONS

8 ounces nuts (1½ cups whole almonds or smoked almonds, 1 cup plus 2 tablespoons pistachios, or 1½ cups toasted and blanched whole hazelnuts [see Note, page 55])

2½ cups confectioners' sugar

¾ cup egg whites (from 6 to 7 large eggs), at room temperature

¼ teaspoon fine sea salt

½ cup plus 2 tablespoons granulated sugar

A few drops of food coloring (optional)

1 batch of ice cream of your choice, slightly softened

For the macaroons:

Line a large baking sheet with parchment paper. Using a 3-inch biscuit or cookie cutter as a guide, trace 12 circles on the parchment (this will ensure that the macaroons are the same size and will match when paired up). Turn the sheet of parchment over.

Grind the nuts with ¼ cup of the confectioners' sugar in a food processor until a fine nut flour forms; do not allow the mixture to become a paste. Add the remaining 2¼ cups confectioners' sugar and pulse just until incorporated. If necessary, strain the mixture through a sieve and discard any large pieces of nuts.

Whip the egg whites and salt in the bowl of a stand mixer with the whisk attachment until frothy. (Or use a hand mixer and a large bowl.) While the mixer is running, slowly add the granulated sugar, about 1 tablespoon at a time, and whip until the meringue is shiny and holds medium peaks, about 5 minutes.

Using a rubber spatula, fold in the almond mixture one-third at a time until thoroughly combined. Without food coloring, the cookies will be a light golden color. If you want more colorful cookies, fold in food coloring a few drops at a time until the desired intensity is reached.

Fit a pastry bag with a ¼-inch plain tip and fill the bag halfway with the batter. (If you don't have a pastry bag, use a plastic freezer bag. Fill the bag, press out excess air, and seal, then cut about ⅟₁₆ inch off one of the corners to create a "tip" from which to pipe.) Holding the bag upright, pipe macaroons inside the traced circles in a spiral, beginning in the center of the circle and working your way out.

Let the cookies sit at room temperature for 30 minutes to dry. This will create the signature crisp crust on the outside of the macaroon.

Preheat the oven to 300°F.

Bake the cookies for 18 to 20 minutes, rotating the tray halfway through, until they have risen slightly and look crisp and set on top. Remove from the oven and let cool completely.

Slide the parchment sheet of macaroons onto a cookie sheet and freeze; once they are frozen, transfer to a freezer bag or storage container. Be careful: macaroons are delicate. They can be frozen for up to 1 month.

To assemble the sandwiches:

Place 6 frozen macaroons upside down on a work surface. One at a time, place a small scoop of ice cream on each cookie and top with another cookie. Gently press the cookies together until the ice cream comes to the edges of the macaroons. Wrap in wax paper, parchment, or plastic wrap and freeze. Sealed in an airtight container, the sandwiches will keep for up to 2 weeks.

Note: To toast and blanch (peel) hazelnuts, spread the nuts on a baking sheet and toast in a preheated 350°F oven for 10 minutes, or until fragrant and lightly browned. Wrap the nuts in a kitchen towel and rub off as much of the skin as you can. Let cool completely.

CHOCOLATE MACAROONS

● ● ● ● ● ● ● ● ● ●● ●

To make chocolate cookies, add 3 tablespoons unsweetened cocoa powder to the confectioners' sugar and almond mixture.

DURING SUMMER, everything is bathed in light and everyone is full of energy. The landscape is saturated with color throughout the long days—in June, the sun doesn't set until almost 10:00 p.m. Evenings are filled with cycling, rambling walks, and visits to the park. Our ice creams reflect summer's brightness, with flavors spiked with berries, peppermint, cucumbers, and sweet corn.

The farmers arrive early every Saturday morning at the North Market, hauling the week's bounty of flavorful produce and Technicolor garden flowers. Peaches, apricots, raspberries, and watermelons come at the peak of summer, joining a cornucopia of vegetables that includes heirloom tomatoes, beets, zucchini, and squash. There are so many colors and flavors, and I like pairing flavors based on where they lie on the color wheel.

I think in color. It would be easy to fill up our display cases with tan, brown, and white—the colors of most of our ice creams. It was a conscious decision to complement those neutrals with pops of currant, pistachio, lavender, and bright yellow curry. In the summer especially, I find myself at the color wheel for inspiration. I've never come up with a bad combination that way. Yellow sweet corn and purple black raspberries was the first combo (yellow and purple, complementary colors, are across from each other on the wheel; see page 62). One of my favorite ingredients, red beets, is paired with orange zest—their hues are next to each other on the color wheel. The ice cream (see page 70) is a subtle tweak on the original inspiration, a lemon beet ravioli I had in Brooklyn. Our Black Plum and Black Currant Lambic Sorbet (see page 87) and our Roasted Pistachio Ice Cream (page 40) are examples of monochromatic color palettes using varying hues of the same colors. Each of these flavors was inspired, in part, by where the colors of the ingredients are on the color wheel. Summer is the perfect time for such inspirations.

The energy among the merchants in the North Market is tangible. There's a quickness of step, a purpose to each stride. And it's hard to walk through the farmers' market with efficiency. Familiar faces and crowds of people hauling armfuls of leafy greens block your way. You're sure to catch chef Alana Shock passionately snatching up a farmer's entire inventory for her restaurant's dinner service that week. At Alana's Food and Wine she'll use every bit of it, putting some away for winter, as she has done since I met her years ago.

Our kitchen is in high gear, peeling, chopping, and pureeing. First berries, then mint, apricots, plums, and eventually cucumbers, melons, celery, and beets. It's a mad dash to get them into ice cream—we don't have much room in our kitchen or cooler to store them.

At our shops, the lists of flavors on the enormous chalkboards sometimes change hourly with the growing season. When our day is done, Charly and I take our children, Greta and Dashiell, for a swim or a bike ride and picnic, and afterward we stand in line with everyone else to wait for ice cream.

LOCAL & WAYWARD

Ohio is one of just five states that boast more than 50 percent prime farmland. The rich soil is naturally fertile and built to yield a variety of crops. I take it for granted sometimes, but making artisanal ice cream requires only that I cultivate relationships with nearby farmers who grow what we're looking for, or know someone near us who is. Our Ohio farm-derived ice cream, like fine wine, reflects its terroir and the personality of its makers.

• • • • • •

But using locally grown crops is not part of a self-righteous, chest-beating stance. We simply use what tastes best. If we had to use strawberries shipped from California rather than strawberries harvested on various farms in central Ohio, we simply wouldn't make Roasted Strawberry & Buttermilk Ice Cream (page 30). If we couldn't get our hands on black walnuts from southeast Ohio, we wouldn't make Black Walnut Divinity Ice Cream (page 168). And if we couldn't get the leaves of the lovely peppermint that stokes our Backyard Mint Ice Cream (page 72), we wouldn't waste our time.

Adam Welly and Jaime Moore of Wayward Seed Farm, Val Jorgensen at Jorgensen Farms, and Chris Schmiel at Integration Acres, all suppliers of ours for the last several years, grow some of the best ingredients we've tasted. They are entrepreneurs driven by quality, heritage, sustainability, and innovation. We started out buying small crates of their produce, nuts, and herbs. Now we buy entire fields of blueberries, strawberries, and melons from Wayward Seed; hundreds of pounds of walnuts and elderberries from Integration Acres; and bushels of herbs from Jorgensen Farms.

Adam and Jaime, Chris, and Val work with me to select varieties of fruits, vegetables, and other crops ideally suited for ice cream making. One of our favorite fruits from Adam and Jaime is intensely flavorful heirloom watermelon, studded with big black seeds. The flavor of the sorbet we make with their "Disco" melons, as Adam calls this 1970s-spawned variety, is outta sight. We toss some of the seeds back into the final product to remind people that they are eating something that owes its existence to, you know, a watermelon.

Chris operates a small goat farm and founded a long-running festival centered on Ohio's official native fruit, the pawpaw. He knows everyone in southeast Ohio and is working on befriending everyone beyond that Appalachian territory. Chris is an invaluable resource, and the customers who clamor for our Black Walnut Divinity Ice Cream have him to thank for that old-timey flavor. And Val Jorgensen's 65-acre organic farm yields not only top-drawer honey and lamb, but also the best strain of Robert Mitchum peppermint ever.

The best thing, though, about working with Adam and Jaime, Chris, Val, and others with strong ties to the state is that if we don't know where to get a certain tasty ingredient, they always know someone who does. From the Columbus city limits to the state line in every direction has become a sort of garden for us.

SWEET CORN &
BLACK RASPBERRY ICE CREAM

A sublime summer match — initial hits of milky sweet corn give way to the floral nose of sweet black raspberry.

Ohio sweet corn is milky-tasting and shockingly sweet. I like to eat it raw straight off the truck. We add sea salt and fresh cream and milk to make a delightful peak-harvest ice cream, then swirl it with black raspberry sauce. This is the taste of summertime in Ohio, especially in Columbus, where this flavor has had a loyal following since I first made it over ten years ago.

Sweet corn ice cream is delicious on its own. My initial reason for adding black raspberries was visual, but black raspberries offer a perfect sweet-tart perfume to the flavor (complementary colors often make complementary flavors). If you can't find good black raspberries for the sauce (some years they are all seeds—don't bother), use half blackberries and half red raspberries, so the color is still a deep purple to complement the yellow corn.

Pairs well with: Blue corn cakes with lots of powdered sugar and Queen City Cayenne Ice Cream (page 160). Bumbleberry crumble. Honey Butterscotch Sauce (page 202).

Makes a generous 1 quart

1 ear sweet corn, husked

2 cups whole milk

1 tablespoon plus 1 teaspoon cornstarch

1½ ounces (3 tablespoons) cream cheese, softened

¼ teaspoon fine sea salt

1¼ cups heavy cream

⅔ cup sugar

2 tablespoons light corn syrup

Black Raspberry Sauce (page 196)

TASTING NOTES

_____

_____

_____

_____

_____

_____

PREP Slice the kernels from the corn cob, then "milk" the cob by scraping it with the back of your knife to extract the liquid; reserve the kernels and liquid.

Mix about 2 tablespoons of the milk with the cornstarch in a small bowl to make a smooth slurry.

Whisk the cream cheese and salt in a medium bowl until smooth.

Fill a large bowl with ice and water.

COOK Combine the remaining milk, the cream, sugar, corn and juices, and corn syrup in a 4-quart saucepan, bring to a rolling boil over medium-high heat, and boil for 4 minutes. Remove from the heat and force the mixture through a sieve into a bowl, leaving the corn "cases" behind. Return the mixture to the saucepan and gradually whisk in the cornstarch slurry. Bring back to a boil over medium-high heat and cook, stirring with a heatproof spatula, until slightly thickened, about 1 minute. Remove from the heat.

CHILL Gradually whisk the hot milk mixture into the cream cheese until smooth. Pour the mixture into a 1-gallon Ziploc freezer bag and submerge the sealed bag in the ice bath. Let stand, adding more ice as necessary, until cold, about 30 minutes.

FREEZE Pour the ice cream base into the frozen canister and spin until thick and creamy.

Pack the ice cream into a storage container, alternating it with layers of the black raspberry sauce and ending with a spoonful of sauce; do not mix. Press a sheet of parchment directly against the surface, and seal with an airtight lid. Freeze in the coldest part of your freezer until firm, at least 4 hours.

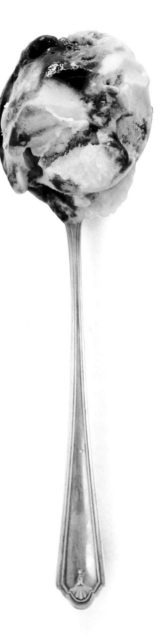

KONA STOUT ICE CREAM

Roasted malt and coffee beans impart a chocolaty nose to this rich, refreshing ice cream.

Use the darkest beer you can find. A dark stout packs a lot of flavor without adding too much water to the ice cream, so it stays creamy and flavorful. We use two stars of the Columbus brewing world, Russian Imperial Stout from Barley's Alehouse and Kona coffee from Stauf's Coffee Roasters. Barley's is right across the parking lot from the North Market, and I've used its brews since my earliest days in ice cream experimentation.

I grew up with Stauf's coffee, and I use their Kona because it's my favorite to drink. But you can use whichever coffee you like. Just remember that the darker the roast, the richer the flavor, so you may need to account for that when you decide how much coffee to use in the recipe.

We make this flavor each year at Father's Day and continue all summer long. It's a great hot-weather treat, bitter and as refreshing as a cold beer or an iced coffee. My kitchen notes say, "Off-the-hook good." I think you'll agree.

Pairs well with: Chocolate cake. Blackstrap-molasses gingerbread. Whiskey. Barbecue. Your dad.

Makes about 1 quart

2 cups whole milk

1½ tablespoons cornstarch

1½ ounces (3 tablespoons) cream cheese, softened

⅛ teaspoon fine sea salt

1¼ cups heavy cream

⅔ cup sugar

2 tablespoons light corn syrup

2 tablespoons dark-roast Kona coffee beans, coarsely ground

½ cup Barley's Russian Imperial Stout or other very dark stout

TASTING NOTES

_____

_____

_____

_____

_____

_____

PREP Mix about 2 tablespoons of the milk with the cornstarch in a small bowl to make a smooth slurry.

Whisk the cream cheese and salt in a medium bowl until smooth.

Fill a large bowl with ice and water.

COOK Combine the remaining milk, the cream, sugar, and corn syrup in a 4-quart saucepan, bring to a rolling boil over medium-high heat, and boil for 4 minutes. Remove from the heat, add the coffee, and let steep for 5 minutes.

Strain the milk mixture through a sieve lined with a layer of cheesecloth. Squeeze the coffee in the cheesecloth to extract as much liquid as possible, then discard the grounds.

Return the cream mixture to the saucepan and gradually whisk in the cornstarch slurry. Bring back to a boil over medium-high heat and cook, stirring with a rubber spatula, until slightly thickened, about 1 minute. Remove from the heat.

CHILL Gradually whisk the hot milk mixture into the cream cheese until smooth. Add the stout and blend well.

Pour the mixture into a 1-gallon Ziploc freezer bag and submerge the sealed bag in the ice bath. Let stand, adding more ice as necessary, until cold, about 30 minutes.

FREEZE Pour the ice cream base into the frozen canister and spin until thick and creamy.

Pack the ice cream into a storage container, press a sheet of parchment directly against the surface, and seal with an airtight lid. Freeze in the coldest part of your freezer until firm, at least 4 hours.

GOAT CHEESE ICE CREAM
WITH ROASTED RED CHERRIES

Sweet-tart roasted Michigan cherries are balanced by pure, tangy goat cheese. Like a cherry cheesecake, but better.

Goat Cheese Ice Cream pairs with many fruits, but we make it two ways: roasted red cherries go into our spring and summer version, and in the fall and winter we switch to Cognac figs. The cherry or fig compote can also be served on top of the ice cream, rather than layered into it.

The combination of these flavors reminds me of the center of a cheese Danish. Roasted red cherries burst with concentrated sweet cherry flavor. Dried figs plumped with sugar and Cognac are warmly decadent and sweet. Serve either with a glass of tawny port or Banyuls.

As for the goat cheese, find a fresh, locally prepared cheese if you can; it will be the most flavorful and have the cleanest finish. Jean Mackenzie, who supplies our goat cheese, makes some of the best I have ever had.

Pairs well with: Chocolate. Ice wine. Toasted hazelnuts.

Makes a generous 1 quart

2 cups whole milk

1 tablespoon plus 1 teaspoon cornstarch

½ cup (about 4 ounces) fresh goat cheese

1½ ounces (3 tablespoons) cream cheese, softened

¼ teaspoon fine sea salt

1¼ cups heavy cream

⅔ cup sugar

¼ cup light corn syrup

Roasted Cherries (page 196)

TASTING NOTES

_____

_____

_____

_____

_____

_____

PREP Mix about 2 tablespoons of the milk with the cornstarch in a small bowl to make a smooth slurry. Whisk the goat cheese, cream cheese, and salt in a medium bowl until smooth. Fill a large bowl with ice and water.

COOK Combine the remaining milk, the cream, sugar, and corn syrup in a 4-quart saucepan, bring to a rolling boil over medium-high heat, and boil for 4 minutes. Remove from the heat, and gradually whisk in the cornstarch slurry. Bring the mixture back to a boil over medium-high heat and cook, stirring with a rubber spatula, until slightly thickened, about 1 minute. Remove from the heat.

CHILL Gradually whisk the hot milk mixture into the cream cheese mixture until smooth. Pour the mixture into a 1-gallon Ziploc freezer bag and submerge the sealed bag in the ice bath. Let stand, adding more ice as necessary, until cold, about 30 minutes.

FREEZE Pour the ice cream base into the frozen canister and spin until thick and creamy. Pack the ice cream into a storage container, alternating it with layers of the cherries and ending with a spoonful of cherries; do not mix. Press a sheet of parchment directly against the surface, and seal with an airtight lid. Freeze in the coldest part of your freezer until firm, at least 4 hours.

**Goat Cheese Ice Cream
with Cognac Figs**

Make and freeze the ice cream
as directed, then pack it into the
storage container, substituting
Cognac Fig Sauce (page 195)
for the cherries.

BACKYARD MINT ICE CREAM

Bright and sweet-scented muddled mint and fresh cream — completely refreshing.

When I set out to make a fresh mint ice cream, I was looking for peppermint rather than spearmint. Peppermint is sweeter and more refreshing.

Through my search, I met Val Jorgensen, who owns a beautiful farm outside Columbus where she grows herbs, wildflowers, and pear trees; keeps bees; and raises sheep. Val and I worked together over several summers to find the perfect mint for our ice cream. We finally settled on a cool black peppermint with the strange official name of Robert Mitchum Mint. This varietal has a strong, sweet peppermint scent, and it also has a high concentration of oils, which are essential to a flavorful ice cream.

To flavor our ice cream, we roughly tear mint leaves, then cold-soak them in the ice cream base overnight. Tearing the mint bruises the leaves and opens the oil pockets, releasing the scent into the cream. Don't care for mint? You can substitute any fresh herb.

Pairs well with: Dark chocolate, of course (bar or "freckles"—see "Freeze" on page 105). Chocolate fudge cookies, for ice cream sandwiches. Rum or whiskey and some seltzer, for an interesting float.

Makes about 1 quart

2 cups whole milk

1 tablespoon plus 1 teaspoon cornstarch

1½ ounces (3 tablespoons) cream cheese, softened

⅛ teaspoon fine sea salt

1¼ cups heavy cream

⅔ cup sugar

2 tablespoons light corn syrup

A large handful of fresh mint from your backyard or farmers' market, leaves roughly torn into small pieces

TASTING NOTES

_____

_____

_____

_____

_____

_____

PREP Mix about 2 tablespoons of the milk with the cornstarch in a small bowl to make a smooth slurry.

Whisk the cream cheese and salt in a medium bowl until smooth.

Fill a large bowl with ice and water.

COOK Combine the remaining milk, the cream, sugar, and corn syrup in a 4-quart saucepan, bring to a rolling boil over medium-high heat, and boil for 4 minutes. Remove from the heat, and gradually whisk in the cornstarch slurry.

Bring the mixture back to a boil over medium-high heat and cook, stirring with a heatproof spatula, until slightly thickened, about 1 minute. Remove from the heat.

CHILL Gradually whisk the hot milk mixture into the cream cheese until smooth. Add the mint. Pour the mixture into a 1-gallon Ziploc freezer bag and submerge the sealed bag in the ice bath. Let stand, adding more ice as necessary, until cold, about 30 minutes.

Refrigerate to steep for 4 to 12 hours.

FREEZE Strain out the mint. Pour the ice cream base into the frozen canister and spin until thick and creamy.

Pack the ice cream into a storage container, press a sheet of parchment directly against the surface, and seal with an airtight lid. Freeze in the coldest part of your freezer until firm, at least 4 hours.

CELERY ICE CREAM
WITH CANDIED GINGER AND RUM-PLUMPED GOLDEN RAISINS

Celery imparts the aroma of rye; potent candied ginger and rum-soaked raisins, judiciously strewn throughout, add an exotic punch.

Celery and rum raisins are a really tasty late-harvest combination. We make this with ginger or without, depending on our mood. If you buy celery from a farmers' market or grow your own, you will notice that the dark green leaves have a very strong celery flavor and they also have a not-unpleasant mouth-numbing quality. Sometimes I ask Adam, who grows our celery, to pull it early before the stalks have fully grown, when the plant is all leaves, because they have so much flavor.

If you can't find celery with deep green leaves at your farmers' market, you can use celery seeds crushed with a mortar and pestle. You will get great results either way.

Note that if made with celery leaves, the ice cream base must steep for at least 4 hours.

Pairs well with: Ginger ale, for a late-harvest float.

Makes about 1 quart

2 cups whole milk

1 tablespoon plus 1 teaspoon cornstarch

1½ ounces (3 tablespoons) cream cheese, softened

⅛ teaspoon fine sea salt

1¼ cups heavy cream

⅔ cup sugar

2 tablespoons light corn syrup

A large bunch of dark green celery leaves, finely chopped (and/or 1 teaspoon celery seeds, pounded lightly in a mortar with the pestle)

Rum-Plumped Golden Raisins (page 195)

2 tablespoons finely diced candied ginger

TASTING NOTES

_____

_____

_____

_____

_____

PREP Mix about 2 tablespoons of the milk with the cornstarch in a small bowl to make a smooth slurry.

Whisk the cream cheese and salt in a medium bowl until smooth.

Fill a large bowl with ice and water.

COOK Combine the remaining milk, the cream, sugar, and corn syrup in a 4-quart saucepan, bring to a rolling boil over medium-high heat, and boil for 4 minutes. Remove from the heat, and gradually whisk in the cornstarch slurry.

Bring the mixture back to a boil over medium-high heat and cook, stirring with a heatproof spatula, until slightly thickened, about 1 minute. Remove from the heat.

CHILL Gradually whisk the hot milk mixture into the cream cheese until smooth. Stir in the celery leaves (and/or seeds).

Pour the mixture into a 1-gallon Ziploc freezer bag and submerge the sealed bag in the ice bath. Let stand, adding more ice as necessary, until cold, about 30 minutes.

If using celery leaves, allow the ice cream base to steep for 4 to 12 hours in the refrigerator.

FREEZE If using celery leaves, strain them out. Pour the ice cream base into the frozen canister and spin until thick and creamy. Drain the raisins and mix with the candied ginger.

Pack the ice cream into a storage container, folding in the raisins and ginger as you go. Press a sheet of parchment directly against the surface, and seal with an airtight lid. Freeze in the coldest part of your freezer until firm, at least 4 hours.

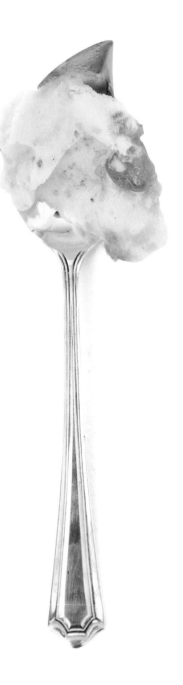

SWEET BASIL & HONEYED PINE NUT ICE CREAM

Sweet basil-infused cream with subtle anise notes; honey-coated pine nuts add the right crunch.

Here's one of those surprising ice cream flavors inspired by a savory dish. It's one of the straight-from-the-farmers'-market flavors that we've built our reputation on. I like the pine nuts to be an occasional encounter in the ice cream and so I use them sparingly, but feel free to add more to your taste.

Pairs well with: Strawberries. Parmesan tuiles. Olive oil cake.

Makes about 1 quart

2 cups whole milk

1 tablespoon plus 1 teaspoon cornstarch

1½ ounces (3 tablespoons) cream cheese, softened

¼ teaspoon fine sea salt

1¼ cups heavy cream

⅔ cup sugar

2 tablespoons light corn syrup

A large handful of fresh basil leaves, roughly torn into small pieces

⅓ cup Honey Pine Nut Pralines (page 194)

TASTING NOTES

_____

_____

_____

_____

_____

PREP Mix about 2 tablespoons of the milk with the cornstarch in a small bowl to make a smooth slurry.

Whisk the cream cheese and salt in a medium bowl until smooth.

Fill a large bowl with ice and water.

COOK Combine the remaining milk, the cream, sugar, and corn syrup in a 4-quart saucepan, bring to a rolling boil over medium-high heat, and boil for 4 minutes. Remove from the heat and gradually whisk in the cornstarch slurry.

Bring the mixture back to a boil over medium-high heat and cook, stirring with a heatproof spatula, until slightly thickened, about 1 minute. Remove from the heat.

CHILL Gradually whisk the hot milk into the cream cheese until smooth. Add the basil.

Pour the mixture into a 1-gallon Ziploc freezer bag and submerge the sealed bag in the ice bath. Let stand, adding more ice as necessary, until cold, about 30 minutes.

FREEZE Strain out the basil. Pour the ice cream base into the frozen canister and spin until thick and creamy.

Pack the ice cream into a storage container, folding in the honey pine nut pralines as you go. Press a sheet of parchment directly against the surface and seal with an airtight lid. Freeze in the coldest part of your freezer until firm, at least 4 hours.

CUCUMBER, HONEYDEW, & CAYENNE FROZEN YOGURT

Japanese cucumbers and sweet honeydew melon meet cool yogurt and cream with a kick of cayenne.

This might be my favorite summer flavor. The cucumber gives it a cleansing, slightly bitter finish, while the honeydew adds a sweet, almost oaky Chardonnay fragrance. The yogurt cools it and the cayenne adds just a bit of heat for some dimension. If you are having a late-summer party and there is spice on the menu, this would be a great dessert.

Cayenne sometimes is added (in very small amounts) to ginger ale to give it just a little kick. Don't be afraid of the cayenne—it can create a bit of drama, and if nothing else, that's good for conversation at the sleepy end of a big meal.

Pairs well with: Bangkok Peanut Ice Cream (page 166). Crushed peanuts. Lemongrass Dry Soda or tequila.

Makes a generous 1 quart

FROZEN YOGURT BASE

1 quart plain low-fat yogurt

1½ cups whole milk

2 tablespoons cornstarch

2 ounces (4 tablespoons) cream cheese, softened

½ cup heavy cream

⅔ cup sugar

¼ cup light corn syrup

CUCUMBER-HONEYDEW SYRUP

1 medium slice honeydew (about ⅛ medium melon)

½ Japanese cucumber

¼ cup sugar

⅛ teaspoon cayenne pepper

TASTING NOTES

_____

_____

_____

_____

_____

_____

ADVANCE PREP

For the strained yogurt:

Fit a sieve over a bowl and line it with two layers of cheesecloth. Pour the yogurt into the sieve, cover with plastic wrap, and refrigerate for 6 to 8 hours to drain. Discard the liquid, and measure out 1¼ cups of the strained yogurt; set aside.

PREP

For the cucumber-honeydew syrup:

Slice the rind from the melon. Cut the flesh into chunks and puree in a food processor. Measure out ⅓ cup honeydew puree.

Peel the cucumber, halve lengthwise, and scoop out the seeds. Cut into chunks and puree in the food processor. Measure out ¼ cup cucumber puree.

Combine the honeydew, cucumber, sugar, and cayenne in a small saucepan and warm over medium heat, stirring, until the sugar dissolves; do not boil. Remove from the heat and let cool.

Mix about 3 tablespoons of the milk with the cornstarch in a small bowl to make a smooth slurry. Whisk the cream cheese in a medium bowl until smooth. Fill a large bowl with ice and water.

COOK Combine the remaining milk, the cream, sugar, and corn syrup in a 4-quart saucepan, bring to a rolling boil over medium-high heat, and boil for 4 minutes. Remove from the heat, and gradually whisk in the cornstarch slurry.

Bring the mixture back to a boil over medium-high heat and cook, stirring with a heatproof spatula, until slightly thickened, about 1 minute. Remove from the heat.

CHILL Gradually whisk the hot milk mixture into the cream cheese until smooth. Add the 1¼ cups yogurt and the cucumber-honeydew syrup and whisk until smooth.

Pour the mixture into a 1-gallon Ziploc freezer bag and submerge the sealed bag in the ice bath. Let stand, adding more ice as necessary, until cold, about 30 minutes.

FREEZE Pour the frozen yogurt base into the frozen canister and spin until thick and creamy.

Pack the frozen yogurt into a storage container, press a sheet of parchment directly against the surface, and seal with an airtight lid. Freeze in the coldest part of your freezer until firm, at least 4 hours.

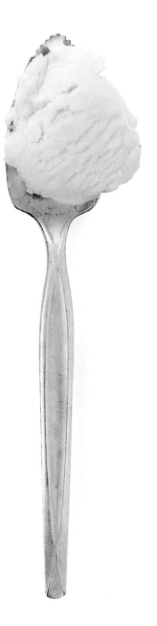

STREET

jen's

SPLENDID ICE C

TREATS

We use our eye-catching trucks to spread new, ready-to-eat, straight-from-the-kitchen Street Treats all over town. You can make our BombeBasticks and Pop Art Push-Ups at home. And, if you have an ice cream truck, by all means serve them direct to the people.

POP ART PUSH-UPS

Bursting with the sweet-tart flavors of the rainbow.

When Columbus's Wexner Center for the Arts was planning its *Andy Warhol: Other Voices, Other Rooms* show in 2008, I was asked to create a confection inspired by Warhol. Drawing on his illuminations of pop culture and his use of striking colors, we decided Pop Art Push-Ups made perfect sense. Kool-Aid, with its vivid palette and ties to pop culture, is the ideal ingredient. The flavors are not so much flavors as they are flavorful colors. The best thing about Pop Art Push-Ups? They're so good that you will sail through time and space and be an eight-year-old, on the street ordering right out of a truck.

PREP

For the frozen yogurt base:
Make the Frozen Yogurt Base, according to the directions on page 192, through the Prep stage.

For the pop art syrup:
Combine the sugar and water in a small saucepan and bring to a boil over medium-high heat, stirring to dissolve the sugar. Remove from the heat and let cool. Add the Kool-Aid to the sugar syrup and stir until dissolved.
    Combine this colorful syrup with the frozen yogurt base.

FREEZE Pour the mixture into the frozen canister and spin until thick and creamy. Using a spoon, pack it into the push-up containers. Cover with the lids and freeze in the coldest part of your freezer until firm, at least 2 hours.

Makes seven to eight 4-ounce push-ups

Frozen Yogurt Base (page 192)

POP ART SYRUP
3 tablespoons sugar

½ cup water

2 packets Kool-Aid Drink Mix

7 to 8 clear 4-ounce push-up molds with lids (see Sources, page 208)

TASTING NOTES

_____

_____

_____

_____

_____

_____

BOMBEBASTICKS

Buttery handmade cones, artfully assembled with ice cream, and encased in Bombe Shell chocolate.

BombeBasticks, our version of the portable sundae cone, are so versatile. Here's an opportunity for your creativity to really soar. Stick to the tried-and-true and re-create the sundae cones of your childhood, or go wild and pair ice creams with one of three Chocolate Bombe Shell options (page 200). You can make them any size you want. If you make tiny cones, then you can make smaller BombeBasticks.

If the chocolate bombe shell is solid, melt gently in a hot water bath (fill bowl with very hot water and place jar of chocolate bombe shell in it), or pulse in the microwave for a few seconds at a time, stirring regularly. You don't want the chocolate to be too hot.

One cone at a time, pour about ¼ cup chocolate into a cone and swirl to coat the interior. Pour the excess back into the melted chocolate, and dip the top ½ inch of the cone into the chocolate. Set the cone upright in a tall glass and place in the freezer to harden. Repeat for remaining cones.

Soften the ice cream to a scoopable consistency. Remove one cone at a time from the freezer and place a scoop firmly on the top—you don't have to fill the cone, just squish it in really well at the opening. Return the cone to the freezer and repeat with the rest of the cones.

Allow to harden for 1 hour.

Coarsely chop nuts, pretzels, chips, or whatever you want to use and spread on a sheet pan.

Remove one cone at a time from the freezer and dip into the liquid chocolate, rolling to coat. Quickly roll in the nuts, if using, and return to the freezer. Freeze until firm.

Serves 6

Chocolate Bombe Shell (page 200)

6 small handmade Ice Cream Cones (page 203)

1 batch of any flavor of ice cream

½ cup toasted nuts, pretzels, or other crunchy interesting bits

TASTING NOTES

_____

_____

_____

_____

_____

_____

2 scoops
of Lemon
Frozen
Yogurt

garnish
with
fresh
herbs

spoon remaining
fruit syrup over
the sundae

FARMERS' MARKET SUNDAE

This ambrosial sundae is eagerly anticipated each summer at our shops. We usually use tawny port, but it works well with almost any wine or spirit. You can add roughly chopped peaches, apricots, or plums, or substitute them for the berries.

Toss the berries with the sugar, honey, and wine in a bowl and let sit for at least 30 minutes and up to 6 hours, to macerate. The berries will create their own lovely syrup.

To assemble the sundaes:
Divide the macerated fruit among 6 plates (or assemble the sundaes in wide-mouthed Mason jars). Place 2 small scoops of frozen yogurt on top of the fruit, then garnish each sundae with a large dollop of whipped cream and an herb sprig.

Makes 6 servings

3 cups blueberries, raspberries, blackberries, halved strawberries, and/or halved pitted cherries

¼ cup sugar

1 tablespoon honey

2 tablespoons tawny port, ice wine, Champagne, or lambrusco or 1 tablespoon Grand Marnier

Lemon Frozen Yogurt (page 46)

Whipped Cream (page 203)

6 fresh herb sprigs, such as mint, basil, or lemon balm

large spoonful of fresh whipped cream

delicious seasonal fruits

White Rum Praline
Sauce (½ cup)

1 big
scoop of
Backyard
Mint
Ice Cream

squeeze
a little
wedge of lime
all over the
praline sauce

OHITO SUNDAE

This summer sundae was inspired by a mojito cocktail. If you've ever had a mojito, you won't be surprised that a muddled mint ice cream works exceedingly well with a muscovado rum sauce. Sundaes are all about the garnishes, and I like this one with a squeeze of lime and a sprinkling of crunchy crystals of turbinado sugar over the whipped cream.

We begin making this sundae every year about midway through summer. Our stores are so tiny that we have to make and deliver the sauce almost daily to each one to keep them stocked for the evening rush. Though we pledge not to run out of fresh-made things, we often run out of the Ohito sauce. The sundae is just that good.

garnish with a sprig of mint to add a bold color

For the white rum praline sauce:
Blend the praline sauce and rum together.

To assemble the sundaes:
Put 1 big scoop or 2 small scoops of ice cream in each bowl or dish and spoon about ⅓ cup sauce over the ice cream. Squeeze a little lime juice over the sauce and top with a generous dollop of whipped cream. Sprinkle the sugar over the whipped cream, and garnish with the mint.

generous dollop of Whipped Cream

Makes 6 servings

WHITE RUM PRALINE SAUCE
Praline Sauce (page 201)

2 tablespoons white rum

Backyard Mint Ice Cream
  (page 72)

1½ to 2 limes, cut into 6 wedges

Whipped Cream (page 203)

2 tablespoons turbinado sugar
  (such as Sugar in the Raw)

6 fresh mint sprigs

TUSCAN SUNDAE
. . .
THE BEST SUNDAE YOU'LL
EVER EAT

OSLO AMBROSIA SUND[E]
. . .
A LOVELY MESS !

AUTUMN IS MY FAVORITE SEASON. The sky is bright blue, and the heat and humidity have relented. If we're fortunate, the weather cooperates right on through November. Although the first day of winter is officially December 21 or 22, our kitchen's Flavor Calendar says autumn lasts through the holidays and the end of the year, and we pull out all the stops.

As summer's heat subsides and daylight lessens, the mood at Jeni's reflects an inner glow. Just as Mother Nature tints the foliage and flowers with the most spectacular hues of her palette, the kitchen staff dips into vivid flavors such as molasses, pumpkin, and apple cider and begins to toy with dazzling autumnal spices such as spicebush berry foraged in Appalachia.

The fall harvest season is one of comfort and abundance. Friends who farm and garden reap the final rewards of their hard labor. The aromas flooding the kitchen are warm and inviting, and if aromas can be cozy, then surely autumn flavors are that—inspiring just a bit more togetherness among the team than during other seasons.

The hustle of summer's over, but our busy shipping season is just beginning. We turn the ovens back on for the season and they will run all through winter. The kettle is always filled with the many chocolate flavors offered this time of year, and the kitchen smells of spices and spirits. The team, composed of so many one-of-a-kind personalities, prepares for December, and our freezers can barely hold enough pints to meet the holiday demand.

In the shops, the Tuscan Sundae (proudly advertised as "the best sundae you'll ever eat") comes back, and customers rush the doors, thanks to Twitter. The art department is busy getting the decorations in place that they have spent months creating. I am taking it all in. With an eye on the holidays, the focus is on family and drinking in all the wonderful flavors.

CHOCOLATE & SHAWN ASKINOSIE

We are a true cow-to-cone ice cream company. When Shawn and his team say they are bean-to-bar chocolate makers, they mean it, too. Their seventy-step process begins with a trip to meet prospective cocoa farmers. Askinosie Chocolate distinguishes itself by developing personal relationships with cocoa farmers and by insisting that they be accountable for their sources. Shawn picks the farmers before he picks the beans. That way, he and the farmers can select which varieties to grow and how to develop the ideal methods for farming and processing them. Now, he is working with farmers in San José del Tambo, Ecuador; Davao City, Philippines; and the Soconusco region of Mexico. His ground-level involvement ensures top quality and flavor.

· · · · ·

The attention to detail doesn't end there. When bags of cocoa beans are delivered to the factory, team members inspect each bag. While roasting the beans, to draw out the unique flavor characteristics, they regularly check on their progress. After roasting, they remove the hulls, revealing the nibs. Some nibs are packaged as is. (Cocoa nibs folded into butterscotch ice cream are like a drug to true chocolate lovers.) The rest are ground into a paste to make cocoa liquor; Askinosie produces its own cocoa butter from the fat in the cocoa liquor. (Most small-batch chocolate makers buy cocoa butter in bulk from industrial chocolate makers.) Then the chocolate-making process begins. After pure cane sugar—the only ingredient Askinosie doesn't make itself—is added, any type of chocolate is possible, from dark chocolates of varying degrees and strength to creamy milk and silky white chocolates.

The final step in the long journey from bean to bar is when Shawn revisits, for example, the cocoa farm in San José del Tambo, to give farmers 10 percent of the net profit from the chocolate made from their beans. The way Shawn sees it, if farmers' profits are based on sales of the chocolate made from their crops, they will work harder to produce the highest-quality beans. Whether you buy your ingredients from local or faraway sources, knowing your suppliers always guarantees better flavor.

I met Shawn in 2008 at Slow Food Nation in San Francisco. He now supplies us with the cocoa and chocolate we use for our chocolate ice cream. The ice cream we make with Askinosie cocoa and chocolate bars is fruity and light in color but pungent. It's delicious the way cheese, wine, and black truffles are delicious. I encourage you to experiment with single-origin bean-to-bar chocolate. A world of flavor will open up to you.

THE DARKEST CHOCOLATE ICE CREAM IN THE WORLD

Mouth-filling, palate-gripping, intense chocolate with a fudge-like texture and a pleasingly dry finish.

This recipe is a result of a career-long quest: packing as much chocolate into ice cream without taking away the ice-creaminess. It is rich, bittersweet, and dense, and the texture is slightly chewy, with extreme chocolate flavor. Folks often say it tastes like the inside of a chocolate truffle.

Always use the best ingredients available, especially when making an ice cream with one singular flavor. Use the best-quality chocolate you can get your hands on. A high-cacao, full-bodied, fruity chocolate will cut through the cream, and the flavor will be more dramatic.

Pairs well with: Absolutely every flavor in this book and just about anything else you can imagine.

Makes a generous 1 quart

CHOCOLATE SYRUP
½ cup unsweetened cocoa powder

½ cup brewed coffee

½ cup sugar

1½ ounces bittersweet chocolate (55% to 70% cacao), finely chopped

ICE CREAM BASE
2 cups whole milk

1 tablespoon plus 1 teaspoon cornstarch

1½ ounces (3 tablespoons) cream cheese, softened

⅛ teaspoon fine sea salt

1 cup heavy cream

½ cup sugar

2 tablespoons light corn syrup

TASTING NOTES

_____

_____

_____

_____

_____

_____

Cocoa Zin Ice Cream
Replace the coffee with ½ cup Zinfandel or other dry red wine.

PREP

For the chocolate syrup:
Combine the cocoa, coffee, and sugar in a small saucepan, bring to a boil over medium heat, stirring to dissolve the sugar, and boil for 30 seconds. Remove from the heat, add the chocolate, and let stand for 5 minutes.

Stir the syrup until smooth. Set aside.

For the ice cream base:
Mix about 2 tablespoons of the milk with the cornstarch in a small bowl to make a smooth slurry. Whisk the cream cheese, warm chocolate syrup, and salt in a medium bowl until smooth. Fill a large bowl with ice and water.

COOK Combine the remaining milk, the cream, sugar, and corn syrup in a 4-quart saucepan, bring to a rolling boil over medium-high heat, and boil for 4 minutes. Remove from the heat and gradually whisk in the cornstarch slurry. Bring the mixture back to a boil over medium-high heat and cook, stirring with a heatproof spatula, until slightly thickened, about 1 minute. Remove from the heat.

CHILL Gradually whisk the hot milk mixture into the cream cheese mixture until smooth. Pour the mixture into a 1-gallon Ziploc freezer bag and submerge the sealed bag in the ice bath. Let stand, adding more ice as necessary, until cold, about 30 minutes.

FREEZE Pour the ice cream base into the frozen canister and spin until thick and creamy.

Pack the ice cream into a storage container, press a sheet of parchment directly against the surface, and seal with an airtight lid. Freeze in the coldest part of your freezer until firm, at least 4 hours.

Dark Chocolate Peppermint Ice Cream

Make the ice cream base as directed. When it is chilled, pour into the frozen canister and turn on the machine. Drip 4 drops of pure peppermint essential oil (see Sources, page 208) through the opening in the top of the machine and spin the ice cream.

SALTY CARAMEL ICE CREAM

Initial notes of burnt sugar give way to a mouthwatering salty-sweet balance.

It was at a French bakery where I worked throughout high school and college that I first heard of salted caramel, called "salty" caramel by a chef in his thick French accent. For years it has been the most popular flavor of ice cream in our stores, accounting for more than 20 percent of sales, and we still make it the way we always have, one batch at a time, the sugar hand-stirred in a copper kettle over an open flame. The reward: no better flavor in the world.

Pairs well with: Apple pie. Chocolate cake. Rhubarb Compote (page 42).

Makes about 1 quart

2 cups whole milk

1 tablespoon plus 1 teaspoon cornstarch

1½ ounces (3 tablespoons) cream cheese, softened

½ teaspoon fine sea salt

1¼ cups heavy cream

2 tablespoons light corn syrup

⅔ cup sugar

2 teaspoons vanilla extract

TASTING NOTES

_____

_____

_____

_____

_____

_____

Gravel Road Ice Cream

In the mood for Salty Caramel with nuts? Add smoked almonds and make Gravel Road.

Reduce the salt in the ice cream to ¼ teaspoon, then make and freeze the ice cream. Pack it into the storage container, layering it with 1 cup coarsely chopped smoked almonds.

Danger! This is the dry-burn technique. I don't add water to the sugar before putting it on the heat, as some chefs do. Caramelizing sugar dry means it goes faster, but you have to watch it more closely and be ready with your cream. Here is an overview of what you are going to do:

Stand over the pan of sugar with a heatproof spatula ready, but do not touch the sugar until there is a full layer of melted and browning liquid sugar on the bottom with a smaller layer of unmelted white sugar on the top. When the edges of the melted sugar begin to darken, use the spatula to bring them into the center to help melt the unmelted sugar. Continue stirring and pushing the sugar around until it is all melted and evenly amber in color—like an old penny. When little bubbles begin to explode with dark smoke, give the sugar another moment and then remove from the heat. Immediately but slowly pour about 1/4 cup of the cream and corn syrup mixture into the burning-hot sugar. Be careful! It will pop and spit! Stir until it is incorporated, then add a bit more cream and stir, then continue until it is all in.

PREP Mix about 2 tablespoons of the milk with the cornstarch in a small bowl to make a smooth slurry.

Whisk the cream cheese and salt in a medium bowl until smooth.

Mix the cream with the corn syrup in a measuring cup with a spout.

Fill a large bowl with ice and water.

COOK Heat the sugar in a 4-quart saucepan over medium heat until it is melted and golden amber in color (see note above). Remove from the heat and, stirring constantly, slowly add a bit of the cream and corn syrup mixture to the caramel: It will fizzle, pop, and spurt. Stir until well combined, then add a little more and stir. Keep adding the cream a little at a time until all of it is incorporated.

Return the pan to medium-high heat and add the milk. Bring to a rolling boil and boil for 4 minutes. Remove from the heat and gradually whisk in the cornstarch slurry.

Bring back to a boil over medium-high and cook, stirring with a heatproof spatula, until slightly thickened, about 1 minute. Remove from the heat. If any caramel flecks remain, pour the mixture through a sieve.

CHILL Gradually whisk the hot milk mixture into the cream cheese until smooth. Add the vanilla and whisk. Pour the mixture into a 1-gallon Ziploc freezer bag and submerge the sealed bag in the ice bath. Let stand, adding more ice as necessary, until cold, about 30 minutes.

FREEZE Pour into frozen canister and spin until thick and creamy.

Pack the ice cream into a storage container, press a sheet of parchment directly against the surface, and seal with an airtight lid. Freeze in the coldest part of your freezer until firm, at least 4 hours.

THE BUCKEYE STATE
ICE CREAM
HONEYED PEANUT ICE CREAM WITH DARK
CHOCOLATE FRECKLES

Rich and salty peanut butter ice cream with the crunch of exceptionally dark chocolate.

Buckeye trees grow throughout Ohio, and candy buckeyes—balls of peanut butter and honey, dipped in chocolate—line the shelves of every bakery, sweet shop, ice cream parlor, and gas station in the state. I understand why: buckeyes are easy to make and undeniably splendid.

Fresh-ground peanut butter tastes better. We get ours from Columbus's Krema Nut Company. I've worked with Krema since I made my first batch of Bangkok Peanut Ice Cream. They have been roasting peanuts and grinding them into butter the old-fashioned way since 1898.

Pairs well with: Extra-Bitter Hot Fudge Sauce (page 201), bananas, and whipped cream.

Makes about 1 quart

2 cups whole milk

1 tablespoon plus 1 teaspoon cornstarch

1½ ounces (3 tablespoons) cream cheese, softened

½ cup unsalted natural peanut butter

½ teaspoon fine sea salt (less if using saltier peanut butter)

1¼ cups heavy cream

⅔ cup sugar

2 tablespoons light corn syrup

2 tablespoons honey

4 ounces chocolate (55% to 70% cocoa), chopped

TASTING NOTES

_____

_____

_____

_____

_____

_____

PREP Mix about 2 tablespoons of the milk with the cornstarch in a small bowl to make a smooth slurry.

Whisk the cream cheese, peanut butter, and salt in a medium bowl until smooth.

Fill a large bowl with ice and water.

COOK Combine the remaining milk, the cream, sugar, corn syrup, and honey in a 4-quart saucepan, bring to a rolling boil over medium-high heat, and boil for 4 minutes.

Remove from the heat, and gradually whisk in the cornstarch slurry.

Bring the mixture back to a boil over medium-high heat and cook, stirring with a heatproof spatula, until slightly thickened, about 1 minute. Remove from the heat.

CHILL Gradually whisk the hot milk mixture into the cream cheese mixture until smooth. Pour the mixture into a 1-gallon Ziploc freezer bag and submerge the sealed bag in the ice bath. Let stand, adding more ice as necessary, until cold, about 30 minutes.

FREEZE Pour the ice cream base into the frozen canister and begin to spin the ice cream.

Meanwhile, melt the chocolate in a double boiler. Remove from the heat and let cool until tepid but still fluid.

When the ice cream is thick and creamy and almost finished, drizzle the melted chocolate slowly through the opening in the top of the ice cream machine and allow it to solidify and break up in the ice cream for about 2 minutes.

Pack the ice cream into a storage container, press a sheet of parchment directly against the surface, and seal with an airtight lid. Freeze in the coldest part of your freezer until firm, at least 4 hours.

STAR ANISE ICE CREAM
WITH CANDIED FENNEL SEEDS

Spicy, fragrant, slightly tangy star anise scents the ice cream, and multicolored, candy-coated fennel seeds add a flavorful crunch.

France, Italy, Greece, India, China, Scandinavia—the flavor of anise is at home in kitchens the world over. Having spent a summer on a small island in Greece and some time in the South of France, where ouzo and pastis are consumed in tiny watering holes, and even toothpaste is anise-flavored, I associate the licorice taste with pleasant memories. It takes me back to those adventures each time I eat it. I love how a glass of pastis is crystal clear when you pour it and how the water you add (and the sugar cube you drop in) clouds it up.

The plump, colorful, candy-coated fennel seeds I get from our local Indian grocery melt into little pockets of color in every bite of this wonderfully festive ice cream.

Note that the ice cream base must steep for at least 4 hours.

Pairs well with: Mangoes. Roasted Pistachio Ice Cream (page 40).

Makes about 1 quart

2 cups whole milk

1 tablespoon plus 1 teaspoon cornstarch

1½ ounces (3 tablespoons) cream cheese, softened

¼ teaspoon fine sea salt

1¼ cups heavy cream

⅔ cup sugar

2 tablespoons light corn syrup

5 whole star anise

½ cup candied fennel seeds (see Sources, page 208)

TASTING NOTES

PREP Mix about 2 tablespoons of the milk with the cornstarch in a small bowl to make a smooth slurry.

Whisk the cream cheese and salt in a medium bowl until smooth.

Fill a large bowl with ice and water.

COOK Combine the remaining milk, the cream, sugar, corn syrup, and star anise in a 4-quart saucepan, bring to a rolling boil over medium-high heat, and boil for 4 minutes. Remove from the heat, and gradually whisk in the cornstarch slurry.

Bring the mixture back to a boil over medium-high heat and cook until slightly thickened, about 1 minute.

CHILL Gradually whisk the hot milk mixture into the cream cheese until smooth.

Pour the mixture into a 1-gallon Ziploc freezer bag and submerge the sealed bag in the ice bath. Let stand, adding more ice as necessary, until cold, about 30 minutes. Refrigerate to steep for 4 to 12 hours.

FREEZE Strain out the star anise. Pour the ice cream base into the frozen canister and spin until thick and creamy.

Pack the ice cream into a storage container, folding in the candied fennel seeds as you go. Press a sheet of parchment directly against the surface and seal with an airtight lid. Freeze in the coldest part of your freezer until firm, at least 4 hours.

ROASTED PUMPKIN 5-SPICE ICE CREAM

A modern classic—rich pumpkin blended with exotic spices, which give the ice cream a light finish and a pleasant tingle.

When I was first getting started at the North Market, my shop was right across from the spice shop, and I spent a lot of time experimenting with different spices and spice blends. When I first smelled Chinese 5-spice, I was reminded of the pumpkin pies that my grandmother made every Thanksgiving. I'm sure this recipe will bring back similar warm memories to you, though 5-spice is something of a departure from the usual nutmeg and allspice medley.

The 5-spice blend that I use is composed of ground cloves, fennel seeds, cinnamon, star anise, and white pepper (authentic 5-spice is made with Szechuan peppercorns, but that is harder to find). Many blends also contain ground ginger; feel free to use whichever one you can find, and add other spices as you like. I often add fresh ginger or candied ginger to this recipe, for a more traditional Thanksgiving flavor.

Pairs well with: Queen City Cayenne Ice Cream (page 160). Gooey Butter Cake Ice Cream (page 164), Goat Cheese Ice Cream with Cognac Figs (page 69). Maple. Cognac.

Makes a generous 1 quart

1 small pie pumpkin or Kabocha, Buttercup, or butternut squash (2 to 3 pounds)

2 cups whole milk

1 tablespoon plus 1 teaspoon cornstarch

1½ ounces (3 tablespoons) cream cheese, softened

¼ teaspoon fine sea salt

¼ cup honey

1¼ cups heavy cream

⅔ cup packed light brown sugar

2 tablespoons light corn syrup

1 tablespoon Chinese 5-spice powder

TASTING NOTES

_____

_____

_____

_____

_____

_____

PREP Preheat the oven to 400°F.

Cut the pumpkin in half and remove the seeds and membranes. Place cut side down on a baking sheet and roast for 30 to 40 minutes, until soft when pierced with a fork. Let cool slightly.

Scoop the flesh into a food processor and puree until completely smooth. Measure out ¾ cup for the ice cream; reserve the rest of the puree for another use.

Mix about 2 tablespoons of the milk with the cornstarch in a small bowl to make a smooth slurry.

Whisk the cream cheese and salt in a medium bowl until smooth. Add the pumpkin puree and the honey and whisk until smooth.

Fill a large bowl with ice and water.

COOK Combine the remaining milk, the cream, sugar, corn syrup, and 5-spice powder in a 4-quart saucepan, bring to a rolling boil over medium-high heat, and boil for 4 minutes. Remove from the heat, and gradually whisk in the cornstarch slurry.

Bring the mixture back to a boil over medium-high heat and cook, stirring with a heatproof spatula, until slightly thickened, about 1 minute. Remove from the heat.

CHILL Gradually whisk the hot milk mixture into the pumpkin mixture until smooth. Pour the mixture into a 1-gallon Ziploc freezer bag and submerge the sealed bag in the ice bath. Let stand, adding more ice as necessary, until cold, about 30 minutes.

FREEZE Pour the ice cream base into the frozen canister and spin until thick and creamy.

Pack the ice cream into a storage container, press a sheet of parchment directly against the surface, and seal with an airtight lid. Freeze in the coldest part of your freezer until firm, at least 4 hours.

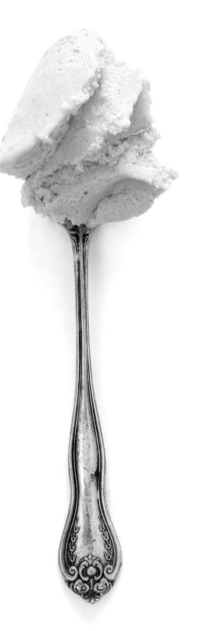

OLIVE OIL ICE CREAM
WITH SEA-SALTED PEPITAS

Rich, verdant cold-pressed extra virgin olive oil meets salty, crispy green pepitas (pumpkin seeds).

Imagine standing before a tree that has been producing fruit and oil for longer than America has been a country. At the Cutrera family estate in Sicily, there are olive trees as old as one thousand years. Breathtaking to behold, these gnarled, knotted trees have large canopies and relatively short, stout trunks. The fresh green olive oil they yield is some of the best I have ever had. It's absolutely spicy when it is first pressed. The flavor of olive oil ranges from nutty and round to green and peppery, depending on the variety and ripeness of the olives, and the climate where the olives were grown.

This is slightly different than the other ice cream recipes; the cream is reduced because the olive oil replaces some of the fat in the ice cream.

You can find roasted and salted pepitas at natural foods stores, Latin American markets, and many supermarkets. If the ones you buy are not salted, heat some olive oil in a skillet over medium heat and toast the pepitas for about 3 minutes, sprinkle with fine sea salt and cool.

Pairs well with: Kumquats. Polenta cake. Figs.

Makes about 1 quart

2 cups whole milk

1 tablespoon plus 1 teaspoon cornstarch

1½ ounces (3 tablespoons) cream cheese, softened

¼ teaspoon fine sea salt

1 cup heavy cream

½ cup sugar

2 tablespoons light corn syrup

¼ cup olive oil

1 cup salted roasted pepitas

TASTING NOTES

_____

_____

_____

_____

_____

_____

PREP Mix about 2 tablespoons of the milk with the cornstarch in a small bowl to make a smooth slurry.

Whisk the cream cheese and salt in a medium bowl until smooth.

Fill a large bowl with ice and water.

COOK Combine the remaining milk, the cream, sugar, and corn syrup in a 4-quart saucepan, bring to a rolling boil over medium-high heat, and boil for 4 minutes. Remove from the heat and gradually whisk in the cornstarch slurry.

Bring the mixture back to a boil over medium-high heat and cook, stirring with a heatproof spatula, until slightly thickened, about 1 minute. Remove from the heat.

CHILL Gradually whisk the hot milk mixture into the cream cheese until smooth. Add the olive oil and whisk until well blended.

Pour the mixture into a 1-gallon Ziploc freezer bag and submerge the sealed bag in the ice bath. Let stand, adding more ice as necessary, until cold, about 30 minutes.

FREEZE Pour the ice cream base into the frozen canister and spin until thick and creamy.

Pack the ice cream into a storage container, folding in the pepitas as you go. Press a sheet of parchment directly against the surface, and seal with an airtight lid. Freeze in the coldest part of your freezer until firm, at least 4 hours.

COGNAC ICE CREAM

Warming alcohol hits first, then the cream and full-flavored butterscotch; almond and brown sugar at the finish.

For a fund-raiser one year, I got to prepare dessert with Lynne Rossetto Kasper. Using the darkest molasses I could find and lots of candied ginger, I made the gingerbread cake from her *The Splendid Table*. I topped this perfect cake with Cognac ice cream and our praline sauce (to which I'd also added a jigger of Cognac). A spark would have set the place ablaze with all that Cognac, but the audience went gaga for the dessert. Now I make it each holiday.

Think of Cognac as the vanilla ice cream of the holiday season. Pumpkin, sweet potato, or pecan pie—it goes with everything in just the right way.

Pairs well with: The holidays.

Makes about 1 quart

2 cups whole milk

1 tablespoon plus 1 teaspoon cornstarch

1½ ounces (3 tablespoons) cream cheese, softened

¼ teaspoon fine sea salt

1¼ cups heavy cream

½ cup sugar

2 tablespoons light corn syrup

¼ cup Cognac

TASTING NOTES

_____

_____

_____

_____

_____

_____

Bourbon Ice Cream with Toasted Buttered Pecans

One of our signature flavors at Jeni's. Substitute bourbon for the Cognac. Pack the ice cream into the storage container, folding in ³⁄4 cup Salty Buttered Pecans (page 194) as you go.

PREP Mix about 2 tablespoons of the milk with the cornstarch in a small bowl to make a smooth slurry.

Whisk the cream cheese and salt in a medium bowl until smooth.

Fill a large bowl with ice and water.

COOK Combine the remaining milk, the cream, sugar, and corn syrup in a 4-quart saucepan, bring to a rolling boil over medium-high heat, and boil for 4 minutes. Remove from the heat, and gradually whisk in the cornstarch slurry.

Bring the mixture back to a boil over medium-high heat and cook, stirring with a heatproof spatula, until slightly thickened, about 1 minute. Remove from the heat.

CHILL Gradually whisk the hot milk mixture into the cream cheese until smooth. Stir in the Cognac.

Pour the mixture into a 1-gallon Ziploc freezer bag and submerge the sealed bag in the ice bath. Let stand, adding more ice as necessary, until cold, about 30 minutes.

FREEZE Pour the ice cream base into the frozen canister and spin until thick and creamy.

Pack the ice cream into a storage container, press a sheet of parchment directly against the surface, and seal with an airtight lid. Freeze in the coldest part of your freezer until firm, at least 4 hours.

Rum Ice Cream with Toasted Coconut

Substitute rum for the Cognac and add ½ cup toasted coconut (see page 194) during the chilling phase or as you pack the ice cream into the storage container.

MAPLE ICE CREAM
WITH SALTY BUTTERED NUTS

Sweet, slightly acidic maple, with a buttery finish.

I grew up on maple syrup that came from my grandparents' trees. I loved the way it soaked my blueberry pancakes into a complete mush. I prefer the lower grades of maple syrup, Grade B or even C, because they have a stronger maple flavor.

For this ice cream, when I can find hickory nuts I throw in some toasted ones. These are native to Ohio and close relatives to their Southern counterpart, the pecan. Smaller than pecans but with a pronounced maple flavor, they are a natural in this ice cream. Otherwise, pecans or walnuts are great here.

Pairs well with: Pumpkin pie. Sweet potato pie. Warm bacon. Belgian waffles (with the ice cream scooped on top).

Makes about 1 quart

2 cups whole milk

1 tablespoon plus 1 teaspoon cornstarch

1½ ounces (3 tablespoons) cream cheese, softened

½ teaspoon fine sea salt

1¼ cups heavy cream

2 tablespoons light corn syrup

1½ cups Grade B or C pure maple syrup, preferably from a small-batch producer

Salty Buttered Hickory Nuts or Pecans (page 194)

TASTING NOTES

_____

_____

_____

_____

_____

_____

PREP Mix about 2 tablespoons of the milk with the cornstarch in a small bowl to make a smooth slurry.

Whisk the cream cheese and salt in a medium bowl until smooth.

Mix the cream with the corn syrup in a measuring cup with a spout.

Fill a large bowl with ice and water.

COOK Bring the maple syrup to a boil in a 4-quart saucepan over medium-high heat. Reduce the heat to medium and continue boiling for 8 minutes, or until it has reduced by one-half and has begun to darken around the edges. Remove from the heat and, stirring constantly, slowly add the cream and corn syrup mixture, then add the remaining milk.

Bring the mixture to a rolling boil over medium-high heat and cook for 4 minutes (the mixture may appear curdled from the acidic maple, but it will come back together in the finished ice cream). Remove from the heat and gradually whisk in the cornstarch slurry.

Bring the mixture back to a boil over medium-high heat and cook, stirring with a heatproof spatula, until slightly thickened, about 1 minute. Remove from the heat.

CHILL Gradually whisk the hot milk mixture into the cream cheese until smooth.

Pour the mixture into a 1-gallon Ziploc freezer bag and submerge the sealed bag in the ice bath. Let stand, adding more ice as necessary, until cold, about 30 minutes.

FREEZE Pour the ice cream base into the frozen canister and spin until thick and creamy.

Pack the ice cream into a storage container, folding in the nuts as you go. Press a sheet of parchment directly against the surface and seal with an airtight lid. Freeze in the coldest part of your freezer until firm, at least 4 hours.

BLACKSTRAP PRALINE ICE CREAM

Blackstrap molasses is slightly acidic, licorice, leather, and ash—an old-fashioned flavor profile.

Blackstrap, a very strong-flavored molasses, comes from the final boiling of sugarcane during processing. The pralines are made with salted pecans shellacked in molasses. The coating will begin to melt in the ice cream, creating pockets of flavor. You can add a pinch of cinnamon or any spice to the pralines if you want, or leave them plain.

Pairs well with: Ginger. Lemon Frozen Yogurt (page 46)—a clash of flavors that works unbelievably well, like treacle pudding with lemon hard sauce, the kind of treat that early Americans would have eaten. Sweet potato soufflé.

Makes about 1 quart

2 cups whole milk

1 tablespoon plus 1 teaspoon cornstarch

1½ ounces (3 tablespoons) cream cheese, softened

¼ teaspoon fine sea salt

1¼ cups heavy cream

½ cup sugar

¼ cup blackstrap molasses

Blackstrap Pralines (page 194)

TASTING NOTES

PREP Mix about 2 tablespoons of the milk with the cornstarch in a small bowl to make a smooth slurry.

Whisk the cream cheese and salt in a medium bowl until smooth.

Fill a large bowl with ice and water.

COOK Combine the remaining milk, the cream, sugar, and molasses in a 4-quart saucepan, bring to a rolling boil over medium-high heat, and boil for 4 minutes (the mixture may appear curdled from the acidic molasses, but it will come back together in the finished ice cream). Remove from the heat, and gradually whisk in the cornstarch slurry.

Bring the mixture back to a boil over medium-high heat and cook, stirring with a heatproof spatula, until slightly thickened, about 1 minute. Remove from the heat.

CHILL Gradually whisk the hot milk mixture into the cream cheese until smooth.

Pour the mixture into a 1-gallon Ziploc freezer bag and submerge the sealed bag in the ice bath. Let stand, adding more ice as necessary, until cold, about 30 minutes.

FREEZE Pour the ice cream base into the frozen canister and spin until thick and creamy.

Pack the ice cream into a storage container, folding in the pralines as you go. Press a sheet of parchment directly against the surface and seal with an airtight lid. Freeze in the coldest part of your freezer until firm, at least 4 hours.

Plum Pudding Ice Cream

This flavor transports me from the middle of Ohio to the center of a Charles Dickens Christmas. You can add fruit and pack it as a terrine (see page 123), then slice it like fruitcake or layer it with Lemon Cream Ice Cream (page 176) for a real old-fashioned treat.

Make and freeze the ice cream. Pack it into the storage container, folding in Plum Pudding Fruits (page 195; drain before using) and ½ cup toasted walnuts, if desired.

OAKVALE YOUNG GOUDA ICE CREAM
WITH VODKA-PLUMPED CRANBERRIES

Nutty and voluptuous, semi-soft young Gouda punctuated with puckery cranberries soaked in small-batch OYO ("oh-why-oh") vodka.

We get our young Gouda from Dale and Jean King at Oakvale Farmstead Cheese, near Columbus, where their family has been milking cows since 1853. Following Dutch cheese-making tradition, they make their Gouda on the same land where they milk their cows, and they always make their cheeses from that day's milking.

For this ice cream, I prefer a young Gouda—it's creamier than an aged cheese, with a mild, nutty flavor, and it melts exceedingly well. You can substitute another semi-soft cheese from your favorite cheese shop.

We soak our cranberries in OYO vodka from MiddleWest Spirits, a young Columbus distillery. Their vodka has a distinctive subtly sweet flavor thanks to Ohio red wheat. Other spirits (grappa, gin, or tequila) can be used or leave the alcohol out completely, if you desire.

Pairs well with: Cookies. Toasted pecans. Aquavit. Grapefruit.

Makes about 1 quart

2 cups whole milk

1 tablespoon plus 1 teaspoon cornstarch

1½ ounces (3 tablespoons) cream cheese, softened

¼ teaspoon fine sea salt

1¼ cups heavy cream

⅔ cup sugar

2 tablespoons light corn syrup

½ cup shredded young Gouda or similar creamy semi-soft cheese

Vodka-Plumped Cranberries (page 195)

TASTING NOTES

_____

_____

_____

_____

_____

_____

PREP Mix about 2 tablespoons of the milk with the cornstarch in a small bowl to make a smooth slurry.

Whisk the cream cheese and salt in a medium bowl until smooth.

Fill a large bowl with ice and water.

COOK Combine the remaining milk, the cream, sugar, and corn syrup in a 4-quart saucepan, bring to a rolling boil over medium-high heat, and boil for 4 minutes. Remove from the heat, and gradually whisk in the cornstarch slurry.

Bring the mixture back to a boil over medium-high heat and cook, stirring with a heatproof spatula, until slightly thickened, about 1 minute. Remove from the heat.

CHILL Gradually whisk the hot milk mixture into the cream cheese until smooth. Add the shredded cheese and whisk until melted and smooth.

Pour the mixture into a 1-gallon Ziploc freezer bag and submerge the sealed bag in the ice bath. Let stand, adding more ice as necessary, until cold, about 30 minutes.

FREEZE Pour the ice cream base into the frozen canister and spin until thick and creamy.

Drain the cranberries. Pack the ice cream into a storage container, layering it with the cranberries as you go. Press a sheet of parchment directly against the surface, and seal with an airtight lid. Freeze in the coldest part of your freezer until firm, at least 4 hours.

GORGONZOLA DOLCE
ICE CREAM
WITH CANDIED WALNUTS

Velvety, buttery, and slightly salty ice cream; black walnuts have the scent of an autumnal forest floor.

Gorgonzola dolce is an ultra-smooth, ultra-high-fat Italian blue cheese. It is milder, sweeter, and creamier than Gorgonzola naturale, which is aged. This ice cream, which is very mild and delicious, was made for dinner parties that go late into the evening. It's essentially both a cheese course and a dessert. I like to recommend that customers mold it in a terrine, then put it in the center of the table on a large wooden cutting board surrounded with nuts, pears, apples, grapes, dried fruits, and plain biscuit cookies and let guests attack it as they would a cheese—using knives and alternating bites of ice cream with fruit and nuts.

Pairs well with: Apple or pear tart. Honey and walnuts.

Makes about 1 quart

2 cups whole milk

1 tablespoon plus 1 teaspoon cornstarch

½ cup (about 2 ounces) softened Gorgonzola dolce

1¼ cups heavy cream

⅔ cup sugar

2 tablespoons light corn syrup

Honey Walnut Pralines (page 194)

TASTING NOTES

_____

_____

_____

_____

_____

_____

PREP Mix about 2 tablespoons of the milk with the cornstarch in a small bowl to make a smooth slurry.

Cream the Gorgonzola with a rubber spatula in a medium bowl until smooth.

Fill a large bowl with ice and water.

COOK Combine the remaining milk, the cream, sugar, and corn syrup in a 4-quart saucepan, bring to a rolling boil over medium-high heat, and boil for 4 minutes. Remove from the heat and gradually whisk in the cornstarch slurry.

Bring the mixture back to a boil over medium-high heat and cook, stirring with a heatproof spatula, until slightly thickened, about 1 minute. Remove from the heat.

CHILL Gradually whisk the hot milk mixture into the Gorgonzola until smooth.

Pour the mixture into a 1-gallon Ziploc freezer bag and submerge the sealed bag in the ice bath. Let stand, adding more ice as necessary, until cold, about 30 minutes.

FREEZE Pour the ice cream base into the frozen canister and spin until thick and creamy.

Pack the ice cream into a storage container, folding in the candied walnuts as you go. Press a sheet of parchment directly against the surface, and seal with an airtight lid. Freeze in the coldest part of your freezer until firm, at least 4 hours.

ICE CREAM TERRINES

I think of ice cream terrines in two ways: as sliceable frozen candy bars, loaded with caramel, chocolate, and sweet, rich vanilla ice cream, and nuts of all varieties, or as an easy way to serve a trio of elegantly assembled flavors, such as three colorful sorbets, which I might place in a large shallow bowl and douse with Champagne like a soup.

An ice cream terrine is a great dessert for a party, since you can serve a lot of people in a short amount of time. Slice, plate, drizzle with sauce, and add a garnish of berries, nuts, or mint—whatever. You can even slice the terrine in advance. Keep the slices in the freezer until dessert time.

We like to assemble our terrines layer by layer with ice cream still soft from the machine. You can use up to three ice creams in a terrine. I love the layered look, but one ice cream also looks great when sliced if it's been blended or coated with interesting bits.

Three batches, or about 3 quarts, of ice cream will fill two 9-by-5-by-3-inch loaf pans (to about an inch from the top).

1. Line each loaf pan with parchment paper, leaving an overhang over both long sides. Fit and crease the paper neatly into the corners of the pan and over the sides. Freeze the pans while you make the first batch of ice cream.

2. Make and spin the first batch of ice cream. One at a time, remove the pans from the freezer and spread the soft ice cream into the pan. If using more than one ice cream, leave equal room for other flavors. Cover with parchment pressed directly against the surface of the ice cream and freeze for at least 1 hour.

3. Make and freeze the second batch of ice cream. Remove the pans, one at a time, from the freezer and peel off the parchment paper from the ice cream. Spread the soft ice cream on top of the first layer, cover with parchment paper, and freeze for at least 1 hour.

4. Make and freeze the third batch of ice cream. Remove the pans, one at a time, from the freezer and peel off the parchment paper from the ice cream. Spread the third batch of soft ice cream on top of the second batch, cover with parchment paper, and freeze until completely frozen.

5. Remove each terrine from the freezer and unmold by running a knife between the short ends of the pan and the ice cream to loosen it. Remove the parchment, and roll the terrine in chopped nuts or candies, if desired. Wrap tightly in parchment and then in plastic wrap to store.

6. To serve, remove the plastic and parchment and slice the terrine. You can do this in advance: layer the slices with parchment squares between them and freeze until dessert time.

SWEET POTATO ICE CREAM
WITH TORCHED MARSHMALLOWS

Pure comfort; spiced sweet potato with cubes of gooey caramelized sweet marshmallows.

When we whip up a batch of this ice cream in our kitchen, we make the marshmallows, cube them, and then spread them on sheet trays and caramelize them with blowtorches. Millions and millions of them (or so it seems). Our customers love this flavor. It's definitely kitschy, but it reminds us of a certain delicious casserole on Midwestern holiday tables, which makes it even better.

Without the marshmallows, this flavor is really great in a Baked Alaska Pie (page 187)—stunning when brought to the Thanksgiving table just from the oven. We are going to try the recipe with purple yams, which can be found fresh or canned in Asian markets, as soon as we can.

Pairs well with: Crushed pineapple. Blackstrap Pralines (page 194). Whiskey.

Makes a generous 1 quart

1½ cups ½-inch cubes peeled jewel yams or sweet potato

2 cups whole milk

1½ ounces (3 tablespoons) cream cheese, softened

¼ teaspoon fine sea salt

¼ teaspoon ground cinnamon, preferably Vietnamese

1¼ cups heavy cream

⅓ cup granulated sugar

⅓ cup packed dark brown sugar

2 tablespoons molasses

1½ cups Vanilla Bean Marshmallows (page 197)

TASTING NOTES

_____

_____

_____

_____

_____

PREP Combine the diced sweet potatoes and milk in a saucepan and bring to a boil. Reduce the heat to low and simmer until the potatoes are soft and easily pierced with a knife, 8 to 10 minutes.

Beat the cream cheese with the salt and cinnamon in a large bowl until smooth.

Fill a large bowl with ice and water.

COOK Once the potatoes are cooked, transfer to a food processor, puree, then return to the pan or puree in the pan using an immersion blender. Add the heavy cream, sugars, and molasses to the potato puree, bring to a rolling boil over medium-high heat, and boil for 4 minutes. Remove from the heat.

CHILL Gradually whisk the hot cream mixture into the cream cheese until smooth.

Pour the mixture into a 1-gallon Ziploc freezer bag and submerge the sealed bag in the ice bath. Let stand, adding more ice as necessary, until cold, about 30 minutes.

While the base is chilling, toast the marshmallows: Spread the marshmallow cubes on a baking sheet. Use a kitchen torch to brown the tops of the marshmallows. Let cool for a few minutes, then shake the pan so the marshmallows turn over. Torch the tops of the marshmallows again and let cool for a few minutes. Continue to shake and torch the marshmallows until all are a fairly uniform lovely brown. Let cool.

FREEZE Pour the ice cream base into the frozen canister and spin until thick and creamy.

Pack the ice cream into a storage container, layering it with toasted marshmallows as you go; reserve one or two and use to decorate the top. Press a sheet of parchment directly against the surface, and seal with an airtight lid. Freeze in the coldest part of your freezer until firm, at least 4 hours.

LIME CARDAMOM FROZEN YOGURT

Tart lime gives way to the tang of yogurt; cardamom, with notes of citrus and pine, adds a blunt floral perfume.

Cardamom is equally at home in sweet and savory preparations. Its delicate balance of spice and aroma, sweet and citrusy, makes it a wonderful addition to everything from curries to baked goods or coffee. In the winter, we make this with a lingonberry compote from Sweden, layering it into the frozen yogurt.

Pairs well with: Lingonberries. Cranberries. Dark chocolate truffles.

Makes a generous 1 quart

FROZEN YOGURT BASE

1 quart plain low-fat yogurt

1½ cups whole milk

2 tablespoons cornstarch

2 ounces (4 tablespoons) cream cheese, softened

½ cup heavy cream

⅔ cup sugar

¼ cup light corn syrup

Zest of 3 limes (reserved from the syrup)

¼ teaspoon ground cardamom

LIME SYRUP

3 to 4 limes

3 tablespoons sugar

TASTING NOTES

_____

_____

_____

_____

_____

_____

ADVANCE PREP

For the strained yogurt:
Fit a sieve over a bowl and line it with two layers of cheesecloth. Pour the yogurt into the sieve, cover with plastic wrap, and refrigerate for 6 to 8 hours to drain. Discard the liquid, and measure out 1¼ cups of the strained yogurt; set aside.

PREP

For the lime syrup:
Using a vegetable peeler, remove the zest from 3 limes in large strips; reserve. Halve the limes and squeeze enough juice to measure ½ cup. Combine lime juice and sugar in a small saucepan and bring to a boil over medium-high heat, stirring to dissolve the sugar. Remove from the heat and let cool.

For the frozen yogurt base:
Mix about 2 tablespoons of the milk with the cornstarch in a small bowl to make a smooth slurry.

Whisk the cream cheese in a medium bowl until smooth.

Fill a large bowl with ice and water.

COOK
Combine the remaining milk, the cream, sugar, corn syrup, and lime zest in a 4-quart saucepan, bring to a rolling boil over medium-high heat, and boil for 4 minutes. Remove from the heat and gradually whisk in the cornstarch mixture.

Bring the mixture back to a boil over medium-high heat and cook, stirring with a heatproof spatula, until slightly thickened, about 1 minute. Remove from the heat.

CHILL
Gradually whisk the hot milk mixture into the cream cheese until smooth. Add the 1¼ cups yogurt, the lime syrup, and cardamom and whisk until smooth.

Pour the mixture into a 1-gallon Ziploc freezer bag and submerge the sealed bag in the ice bath. Let stand, adding more ice as necessary, until cold, about 30 minutes.

FREEZE
Remove the lime zest. Pour the frozen yogurt base into the frozen canister and spin until thick and creamy.

Pack the frozen yogurt into a storage container, press a sheet of parchment directly against the surface, and seal with an airtight lid. Freeze in the coldest part of your freezer until firm, at least 4 hours.

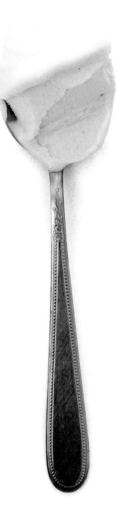

BAKED APPLE SORBET

Baked apples give this sorbet a soft, smooth texture; cinnamon provides warmth.

In October, you can find apple cider at every farmers' market and grocery in Ohio. For that month, it seems it's all we drink—from one of the last crops of the growing season's harvest, apple cider is a treat we cherish. We pick up jugs and jugs from Bill and Vicky Thomas every Saturday at the farmers' market outside the North Market.

Pairs well with: A glass of whiskey. Don't forget the whipped cream!

Makes about 1 quart

1½ cups unfiltered apple cider

6 medium tart apples
    (about 1½ pounds), such as
    Granny Smith, peeled, cored,
    and quartered

¾ cup sugar

½ cup water

¼ cup light corn syrup

1 teaspoon ground cinnamon,
    preferably Vietnamese

1 vanilla bean, split, seeds scraped
    out, seeds and bean reserved

TASTING NOTES

_____

_____

_____

_____

_____

_____

COOK Preheat the oven to 350°F.

Combine all the ingredients, including the vanilla bean and seeds, in a 9-by-13-inch baking dish, tossing to mix.

Cover the dish loosely with foil and bake for 20 minutes, or until the apples are tender. Remove from the oven and let cool. Remove the vanilla bean.

CHILL Puree the apple mixture in 2 batches in a food processor until completely smooth. Force through a sieve. Fill a large bowl with ice and water. Pour the apple mixture into a 1-gallon Ziploc freezer bag and submerge the sealed bag in the ice bath. Let stand, adding more ice as necessary, until cold, about 30 minutes.

FREEZE Pour the sorbet base into the frozen canister and spin just until beginning to have the consistency of very softly whipped cream.

Pack the sorbet into a storage container, press a sheet of parchment directly against the surface, and seal with an airtight lid. Freeze in the coldest part of your freezer until firm, at least 4 hours.

CRANBERRY ROYALE SORBET

A festive, deep-red sorbet with the tart flavors of fresh cranberries and grapefruits.

We love this sorbet in a Champagne float to ring in the New Year. With the cranberries and Ruby Red grapefruits, it's the perfect marriage of holiday flavors. The little pieces of candied cranberries that fall to the bottom of the glass are like bits of confetti. For something different, try this with a dash of sweet, aromatic cardamom.

Pairs well with: Champagne. Oslo Ambrosia (page 136).

Makes about 1 quart

2 grapefruits

One 12-ounce bag cranberries
   (fresh or frozen)

1 cup plus 2 tablespoons water

¼ cup light corn syrup

1½ cups sugar

TASTING NOTES

_____

_____

_____

_____

_____

_____

PREP Using a vegetable peeler, remove 3 large strips of zest from 1 of the grapefruits. Halve the grapefruits and squeeze ¾ cup juice.

COOK Combine the grapefruit juice, zest, cranberries, water, corn syrup, and sugar in a 4-quart saucepan and bring to a boil. Boil just until the cranberries begin to pop open, about 5 minutes. Remove from the heat and let cool.

CHILL Remove the grapefruit zest. If desired, puree the cranberry mixture in batches, or leave unpureed for a chunkier sorbet.

Fill a large bowl with ice and water. Pour the cranberry mixture into a 1-gallon Ziploc freezer bag and submerge the sealed bag in the ice bath. Let stand, adding more ice as necessary, until cold, about 30 minutes.

FREEZE Pour the sorbet base into the frozen canister and spin just until the consistency of very softly whipped cream.

Pack the sorbet into a storage container, press a sheet of parchment directly against the surface, and seal with an airtight lid. Freeze in the coldest part of your freezer until firm, at least 4 hours.

1 Meringue Shell

generous scoop
of Cranberry
Royale

Whipped
Cream .

OSLO AMBROSIA

Our version of *trollkrem,* a famous Norwegian holiday dessert, this sundae is a delightful mess. A joyous union of flavors—raspberry and lingonberry sauce pooled in a sweet, melt-in-your-mouth meringue shell, topped with a scoop of supertart cranberry and grapefruit sorbet. Then we heap on as much hand-whipped fresh cream as possible. Spectacular!

To assemble the sundaes:
Place a meringue shell on each plate. Spoon about 2 tablespoons of the raspberry sauce into the hollow of each meringue, letting it spill over. Place a large scoop of sorbet on top. Top with a double dollop of whipped cream. Top each sundae with a fresh-foraged cloudberry if you happen to have some on hand.

Makes 6 servings

6 Meringue Shells (page 198)

Red Raspberry-Lingonberry Sauce for Sundaes (page 201)

Cranberry Royale Sorbet (page 134)

Whipped Cream (page 203), flavored with a pinch of ground cardamom

Red Raspberry-Lingonberry Sauce

Whipped
Cream

1 scoop of
Salty
Caramel

Vin Santo
Sauce

TUSCAN SUNDAE

This sundae was inspired by a winter trip to Florence. It returns to our menu every year when the weather turns cold, and we advertise it as "the best sundae you'll ever eat." The flavors here are so complementary and play off each other perfectly: the salt and caramelized sugar in the ice cream, the warm honey and Vin Santo sauce—delicious.

Il Santo is an Italian dessert wine that is equally delicious and less than half the price of Vin Santo. Both taste like golden raisins to me.

For the sauce:
Combine the honey, Vin Santo, and star anise, if using, in a small saucepan and heat over low heat until warm. Remove from the heat and discard the star anise, if you used it.

To assemble the sundaes:
Place 2 small scoops of ice cream on each plate or in each bowl. Top each with ⅓ cup warm sauce and garnish with a biscotti, whipped cream, and a cherry.

Makes 6 servings

HONEY AND VIN SANTO SAUCE
1½ cups honey

1½ cups Vin Santo or Il Santo

1 whole star anise (optional)

Salty Caramel Ice Cream
  (page 102)

6 Biscotti (page 198)

Whipped Cream (page 203),
  made with honey

6 Brandied Cherries (page 196)

top with a cherry and Biscotti on the side

PISTACHIO & HONEY

OATMEAL CREME

BAKE SHO

WHEN COLD WEATHER HITS, we have one goal: to blow you away with our flavors. To be irresistible. It's all part of the game. And that is why we have lines out the door—even in February. We know you don't think you are in the mood for ice cream, so we make splendid frozen treats that will change your mind. As gardens and farms lie dormant under a blanket of snow, we busy ourselves with creating ice creams so enticing they draw people out of their homes and into our shops. Coaxing people out into cold weather to eat ice cream is a challenge I relish.

Growing up, I spent winter weekend mornings in the woods, racing our toboggan downhill or walking on the icy creek, knowing that at the day's end I'd make my way to a comforting bonfire that had been beckoning from a hollow in the distance. When we were thoroughly soaked and freezing, we would convene by the fire for lunch, a simple repast of hot cocoa and s'mores. On our way home, we would fall dead asleep, smelly boots still on our feet, oblivious to the 45-minute drive. We slept soundly, content in the knowledge that while we'd been at play, my grandparents had collected more sap from their maple trees, so that we could boil it off for our year's supply of flavorful syrup.

The ice creams in this section are flavors that owe much to the credo "Don't overthink the ingredients, just get right down to the delicious." Gooey, sticky, sweet, warm, comforting—more than any other season, winter is about increasing the amount of pleasure in each bite of the ice cream.

The mood in winter swings wildly from romantic to childish to indulgent. Our shops are in walking neighborhoods, and as soon as a big snowstorm hits, believe it or not, lines

form. The community comes out of hibernation to experience the snow and a glorious winter pastime: walking down a cozy street with an ice cream cone in hand. The fact that it takes longer to melt just gives you more time to enjoy it all. And standing in that line snaking out the door while waiting for ice cream on a frigid, snowy day is one of the greatest ways to meet up with family, neighbors, and strangers soon to be called friends.

Our kitchen bustles in the clear light of winter, ovens on, cozy and warm, fragrant with the aromas of brown butter and of cakes baking. Things are a little slower, more deliberate in the winter—we have the time for it. The traffic in the shops lessens a bit during the post-holiday lull, and we are happy for the short break. I'm in the test kitchen dreaming about the growing season and making plans with farmers. The art department, freshly finished with winter-themed posters and decorations, is already working on spring projects.

Note: *Many of the flavors in this section are meant to be desserts in and of themselves; for these I haven't suggested pairings.*

VANILLA & NDALI

As you might imagine, I have spent considerable time with vanilla. Pure extracts, vanilla pastes, beans from many different places in the world—even synthetic flavorings—I have tried them all, and I never tire of the rich, smoky scent of vanilla beans. Vanilla is one of the most versatile ingredients in my kitchen. I tuck vanilla beans behind my ear or stow them in my pockets. As I write these lines, a bouquet of vanilla beans sits on my desk, filling the room with its heady aroma.

● ● ● ● ●

Vanilla beans are the seed pods of an orchid that grows in tropical climates near the equator. This rare variety requires lots of rain, rich soil, and occasional bursts of sun filtered through a thick canopy of trees. Vanilla farming and production requires tremendous attention and care. Though insects occasionally pollinate the flowers, most of the delicate work of pollination must be done by hand, with a pin or paintbrush and within eight hours of the flower's blooming.

Some nine months later, the beans are harvested. Curing them takes up to six months. First they are blanched in hot water, then "sweated" in wool-lined wooden boxes. From there, the whole beans are packaged and distributed or used to make extract. Knowing about the labor-intensive, highly skilled process that farming and curing vanilla beans demands makes the heady scent of vanilla—the second most expensive spice in the world, after saffron—even more alluring.

Vanilla aficionados often tout beans from Madagascar, Tahiti, and where vanilla beans originated, Mexico. It's true that beans from these locales are of fine quality, with unique and notable characteristics. But I would argue that the beans I import from a small plantation in Uganda are the best in the world.

They are complex and smoky, with prominent notes of honey, jasmine, ylang-ylang, and amber.

As is true of many of the exotic ingredients an ice cream maker or pastry chef relies on, the farming and production of vanilla is often tainted with violence, child labor, and low wages. I believe that flavor is experiential—it doesn't just happen on your tongue, it also happens in your imagination. Knowing that the vanilla I use is grown by a group of farmers paid a living wage for their hard work and skill makes it taste better to me. And I experience a deeper level of appreciation and pleasure when I connect with the people who grow my ingredients.

Several years ago, I read about a small fair-trade farm in Uganda called Ndali Estate. An Englishwoman named Lulu Sturdy runs the farm that her family started decades ago. After inheriting the place from her uncle about ten years ago, Lulu dropped her life as a successful furniture builder in England and moved to Ndali. My kind of gal. When she arrived, she found that the farm was in disarray and losing money. She would have to start over. She began farming coffee, cocoa, cardamom, and bananas and then, vanilla. A government grant helped spur on the vanilla project.

Today, Ndali Estate produces high-quality vanilla beans and pure vanilla extract. Lulu pays the men and women who work for her a living wage, and she pays up to five times the normal price to the fair-trade vanilla farmers who supplement her supply. Feeling we were kindred spirits living on opposite sides of the earth, as I read about her, I dashed off an e-mail expressing my desire to use her beans in my ice creams. I quickly heard from her, but she had discouraging news. Because there was no distributor in the States who carried her vanilla beans, I would have to import them myself—at a minimum order of $5,000.

Ordering $5,000 worth of vanilla beans seemed wholly out of reach for our little company, which at the time was operating out of a little break room off our kitchen. But without even tasting the vanilla, I had determined I would do business with her. I e-mailed her back, promising to place an order soon, and began scheming for ways to get the money.

A few months later, in early 2007, I learned of an artisanal food contest sponsored by the Gallo Family Vineyards. The prize for the winner of each category happened to be $5,000. I entered every category for which we could possibly qualify. I went for the obvious, outstanding dairy and outstanding confectionery, but I also entered our Cherry Lambic Sorbet in the outstanding fruit or vegetable category, just in case. I never thought we would win, but I was sitting on my front porch when I got the call from the judges telling me that our sorbet had won. As soon as I hung up the phone, I raced to the computer and sent Lulu an e-mail: "Send us the beans, we have the money."

Winning that cash prize turned out to be only the beginning of a very long journey to get the beans from Ndali Estate to our kitchen in the middle of the United States. Without the help of a customs lawyer (mistake number one!), it took us months and more than a few snags with customs to manage to import the beans. I'll never forget the day they arrived. The box had been bounced back and forth between Uganda, New York, and Columbus many times, and it showed.

Still, these were the freshest vanilla beans I had ever laid my hands on. As we pried open the battered box in our kitchen and encountered the black mass inside, a honeyed scent filled the air. We began dissecting the beans at once, first cutting off the ends, then slicing them right down the middle. The opened pods revealed syrupy, glossy, tiny seeds that we scraped and plunked, with their pod cases, into a kettle full of slowly heating cream. Each batch of cream got no fewer than forty beans. It all felt so extravagant. After rapidly cooling the cream, we let the beans steep in it overnight. The next day, the cream had thickened like velvety custard. We spun it in our ice cream machines and pulled it out for our first bite. Each scent made an appearance one by one, vanilla followed by honey and fresh Ohio cream. It was the last time we ever spoke of "plain vanilla."

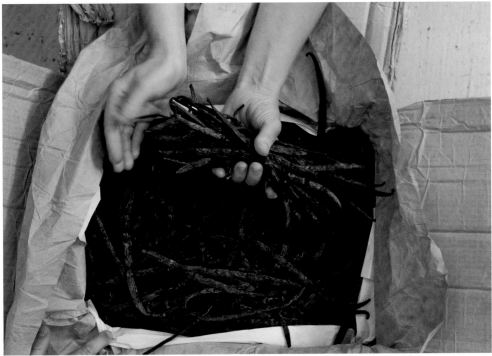

UGANDAN VANILLA BEAN ICE CREAM

The exquisite cream flavor is lifted up and exalted by vanilla's subtle hints of honey, jasmine, leather, and smoke.

With an infinite number of ice cream flavors to make, you might think vanilla would not be high on our list to perfect. Ugandan Vanilla Bean Ice Cream is no ordinary vanilla ice cream. We use a really nice Ugandan vanilla bean (see page 145), but you can use whatever you find that you like. My technique produces not a typical "plain old vanilla," but a richly scented, voluptuous, velvety, and unforgettable vanilla.

Do not hesitate to serve it with some grilled peaches and raspberry sauce for the finest pêche melba imaginable. Of course, vanilla is a staple on cherry pie, and who doesn't have a soft spot for vanilla ice cream with hot fudge, extra whipped cream, and Spanish peanuts (or my favorite, smoked almonds)?

Pairs well with: Is there anything that is not made better with a scoop of vanilla ice cream?

Makes about 1 quart

2 cups whole milk

1 tablespoon plus 1 teaspoon cornstarch

1½ ounces (3 tablespoons) cream cheese, softened

⅛ teaspoon fine sea salt

1¼ cups heavy cream

⅔ cup sugar

2 tablespoons light corn syrup

1 vanilla bean, split, seeds scraped out, seeds and bean reserved

TASTING NOTES

_____

_____

_____

_____

_____

_____

PREP Mix about 2 tablespoons of the milk with the cornstarch in a small bowl to make a smooth slurry. Whisk the cream cheese and salt in a medium bowl until smooth. Fill a large bowl with ice and water.

COOK Combine the remaining milk, the cream, sugar, corn syrup, and vanilla seeds and bean in a 4-quart saucepan, bring to a rolling boil over medium-high heat, and boil for 4 minutes. Remove from the heat and gradually whisk in the cornstarch slurry. Bring the mixture back to a boil over medium-high heat and cook, stirring with a heatproof spatula, until slightly thickened, about 1 minute. Remove from the heat.

CHILL Gradually whisk the hot milk mixture into the cream cheese until smooth. Pour the mixture into a 1-gallon Ziploc freezer bag and submerge the sealed bag in the ice bath. Let stand, adding more ice as necessary, until cold, about 30 minutes.

FREEZE Remove the vanilla bean. Pour the ice cream base into the frozen canister and spin until thick and creamy. Pack the ice cream into a storage container, press a sheet of parchment directly against the surface, and seal with an airtight lid. Freeze in the coldest part of your freezer until firm, at least 4 hours.

Berry Crisp Ice Cream

Another option is Berry Crisp Ice Cream. Make and spin the ice cream, then pack into the storage container alternating it with layers of Roasted Cherries (page 196) or other fruit and Crisp Streusel (page 198). Press a sheet of parchment paper directly against the surface and proceed as directed.

SWANKY COCKTAILS

Swanky cocktails are a great way to ring in the New Year, and they are the right thing to serve at parties throughout the year. Here are some of our favorites made with the sorbets and ice creams in this book. The possibilities are endless. The sorbet or ice cream acts as both the ice and the mixers, and what could be easier than that? This is also a great way to use up leftover ice cream. And look at how pretty they are!

C'BUS 75

1 lemon

1 scoop Riesling-Poached Pear Sorbet (page 130)

1½ ounces Cognac

Champagne

Cut the lemon into wedges and reserve some of the peel for the garnish. Scoop the sorbet into a double Old-Fashioned glass. Pour Cognac over, followed by a squeeze of a lemon. Float with Champagne and add the lemon peel.

DISCO MELON FIZZ

2 small scoops Watermelon Lemonade Sorbet (page 88)

1½ ounces vodka

Soda water

Thin slice of watermelon

Lemon peel

Scoop the sorbet into a tall Collins or highball glass. Pour the vodka over, then tip the glass and slowly fill with soda water. Garnish with the watermelon slice and lemon peel.

APPLE ALEXANDER

1½ ounces brandy

1 scoop Ugandan Vanilla Bean Ice Cream (page 148)

1 scoop Baked Apple Sorbet (page 132)

Nutmeg

Combine the brandy and a spoonful of the ice cream in a shaker; shake until smooth and frothy. Scoop the sorbet into a Champagne coupé. Pour the brandy mixture around—not over—the sorbet scoop. Garnish with freshly grated nutmeg.

LAKESIDE

2 small scoops Cranberry Royale Sorbet (page 134)

Champagne

Scoop the sorbet into a Champagne flute. Top with Champagne. *Salute!*

LOUISVILLE LADY

2 small scoops Backyard Mint Ice Cream (page 72)

2 ounces bourbon

Soda water

Mint sprig

Scoop ice cream into a pint glass. Pour the bourbon over and top with soda water. Garnish with the mint.

BANANA ICE CREAM
WITH CARAMELIZED WHITE CHOCOLATE FRECKLES

Like the best banana pudding, frozen; caramelized white chocolate freckles add crunch and pops of "dulce dulce."

Banana ice cream lends itself to many variations and desserts. Here we pair it with caramelized white chocolate, but you can make it on its own or with dark or milk chocolate freckles (see "Freeze" on page 105). Caramelized white chocolate freckles are like bits of hardened dulce de leche. To make really big chunks of chocolate, use the Caramelized White Chocolate Bombe Shell recipe and pour the cooled mixture into the ice cream as you layer it into the storage container. Chocolate chunks made this way melt just right as you eat them, even when frozen.

We use banana for many things, especially in the winter when other fruits are not in season. A banana ice cream Baked Alaska Pie (page 187), with a layer of Praline Sauce (page 201), may be one of the finest American desserts ever known to man. For ice cream sandwiches, we stuff this flavor, with or without the white chocolate freckles, into macaroons that have a dusting of yellow curry powder on top. In my early days in the market, I put the curry right into the ice cream and also added cashews.

Makes about 1 quart

2 cups whole milk

1 tablespoon plus 1 teaspoon cornstarch

1½ ounces (3 tablespoons) cream cheese, softened

⅛ teaspoon fine sea salt

1¼ cups heavy cream

⅔ cup sugar

2 tablespoons light corn syrup

1 vanilla bean, split, seeds scraped out, seeds and bean reserved

2 ripe bananas

½ recipe Caramelized White Chocolate Bombe Shell (page 200), warmed

TASTING NOTES

_____

_____

_____

_____

_____

_____

PREP Mix about 2 tablespoons of the milk with the cornstarch in a small bowl to make a smooth slurry.

Whisk the cream cheese and salt in a medium bowl until smooth.

Fill a large bowl with ice and water.

COOK Combine the remaining milk, the cream, sugar, corn syrup, and vanilla seeds and bean in a 4-quart saucepan, bring to a rolling boil over medium-high heat, and boil for 4 minutes. Remove from the heat and gradually whisk in the cornstarch slurry.

Bring the mixture back to a boil over medium-high heat and cook, stirring with a heatproof spatula, until slightly thickened, about 1 minute. Remove from the heat.

CHILL Gradually whisk the hot milk mixture into the cream cheese until smooth.

Cut the bananas into chunks and puree in a food processor. Blend the bananas into the hot cream mixture.

Pour the mixture into a 1-gallon Ziploc freezer bag and submerge the sealed bag in the ice bath. Let stand, adding more ice as necessary, until cold, about 30 minutes.

FREEZE Remove the vanilla bean. Pour the ice cream base into the frozen canister and spin until thick and creamy.

When the ice cream is almost ready, melt the white chocolate: scrape it into a bowl, set in a larger bowl, and let stand, stirring occasionally, until warm, liquefied, and smooth.

When the ice cream is ready, drizzle the warm white chocolate into the opening in the top of the machine and continue spinning until it is completely incorporated.

Pack the ice cream into a storage container, press a sheet of parchment directly against the surface, and seal with an airtight lid. Freeze in the coldest part of your freezer until firm, at least 4 hours.

WILD BERRY LAVENDER ICE CREAM

Intense lavender with hints of exotic spices and brambly berry flavors.

Using lavender and other essential oils is a magical and luxurious way to scent ice creams. The aromatic, volatile compounds capture the pure scents, flavors, and characteristics of flowers, rinds, seeds, leaves, wood, and other plant matter. They become encapsulated in cream's butterfat and are often purer in flavor than living or dried plant matter, which can impart bitterness when steeped in cream.

Use only expertly procured, food-grade, single-origin oils (see Sources, page 208). They can be pricey, but just a few drops will richly scent an entire batch of ice cream. I use them around Valentine's Day to make a "bouquet" of ice creams. I also like to add a drop of orange blossom or ylang-ylang to vanilla ice creams to create a deeper yum factor. Here are three of my favorite essential oil flavors.

Makes about 1 quart

BLUEBERRY COMPOTE
½ cup wild blueberries

2 tablespoons sugar

ICE CREAM BASE
2 cups whole milk

1 tablespoon plus 1 teaspoon cornstarch

1½ ounces (3 tablespoons) cream cheese, softened

⅛ teaspoon fine sea salt

1¼ cups heavy cream

⅔ cup sugar

2 tablespoons light corn syrup

2 drops lavender essential oil (see Sources, page 208)

3 drops sweet orange essential oil (see Sources, page 208)

Orange Blossom Ice Cream with Dark Chocolate Freckles

Prep, chill, and cook as directed. Pour the base into the frozen canister and turn on the machine. Add 1 to 3 drops neroli oil and 3 drops blood orange oil through the top, and continue to spin until it is almost finished. Follow the directions under "Freeze" on page 105 for making chocolate freckles. Add in the freckles before packing and freezing.

PREP

For the blueberry compote:
Combine the blueberries and sugar in a small saucepan and bring to a boil, stirring to dissolve the sugar. Remove from the heat and let cool.

For the ice cream base:
Mix about 2 tablespoons of the milk with the cornstarch in a small bowl to make a smooth slurry. Whisk the cream cheese and salt in a medium bowl until smooth. Fill a large bowl with ice and water.

COOK Combine the remaining milk, the cream, sugar, and corn syrup in a 4-quart saucepan, bring to a rolling boil over medium-high heat, and boil for 4 minutes. Remove from the heat and gradually whisk in the cornstarch slurry. Bring the mixture back to a boil over medium-high heat and cook, stirring with a heatproof spatula, until slightly thickened, about 1 minute. Remove from the heat.

CHILL Gradually whisk the hot milk mixture into the cream cheese until smooth. Add the compote and blend well. Pour the mixture into a 1-gallon Ziploc freezer bag and submerge the sealed bag in the ice bath. Let stand, adding more ice as necessary, until cold, about 30 minutes.

FREEZE Pour the ice cream base into the frozen canister and turn on the machine. Drop the essential oils through the opening in the top of the machine, and continue to spin the ice cream until thick and creamy. Pack the ice cream into a storage container, press a sheet of parchment directly against the surface, and seal with an airtight lid. Freeze in the coldest part of your freezer until firm, at least 4 hours.

Ylang-Ylang Ice Cream with Clove and Honeycomb

Prep, chill, and cook as directed. Pour the base into the frozen canister and turn on the machine. Add 2 to 3 drops ylang-ylang oil and 1 drop of clove oil through the top, and continue as directed.

Pack the ice cream into the storage container, layering it with chunks of Honeycomb Candy (page 199). Allow to sit at least overnight or up to a few days, so the honeycomb can begin to melt.

THE MILKIEST CHOCOLATE ICE CREAM IN THE WORLD

Pleasing, milky chocolate with superior creaminess — like a bar of fine Swiss milk chocolate.

I will admit it: I am a milk chocolate junkie. Perhaps I will be excused by chocolate traditionalists because I am a lover of milk and cream above all else. I like chocolate ice cream when it tastes like evaporated milk and chocolate. Here is that recipe. Evaporated milk increases the proteins here and gives the ice cream body, which means there is no need for cream cheese in this recipe.

Makes about 1 quart

1 cup whole milk

1 tablespoon plus 1 teaspoon cornstarch

2 ounces bittersweet chocolate (55% to 70% cocoa)

¼ cup heavy cream

1 cup evaporated milk

⅔ cup sugar

2 tablespoons light corn syrup

⅓ cup unsweetened cocoa powder

¼ teaspoon fine sea salt

TASTING NOTES

_____

_____

_____

_____

_____

_____

Roxbury Road Ice Cream

A darker milk chocolate ice cream with handmade marshmallows, Praline Sauce, and smoked almonds in every bite!

Increase the chocolate to 3 ounces. Make and freeze the ice cream. Pack into the storage container, layering it with ⅔ cup Vanilla Bean Marshmallows (page 197), ½ cup Praline Sauce (page 201), and ½ cup coarsely chopped smoked almonds (or to your taste).

PREP Mix about 2 tablespoons of the milk with the cornstarch in a small bowl to make a smooth slurry.

Chop the chocolate and put it in a medium bowl.

Fill a large bowl with ice and water.

COOK Combine the remaining milk, the cream, evaporated milk, sugar, and corn syrup in a 4-quart saucepan, and bring to a rolling boil over medium-high heat. Add the cocoa, whisking until it is incorporated, and continue boiling for 4 minutes.

Remove from the heat and gradually whisk in the cornstarch slurry.

Bring the mixture back to a boil over medium-high heat and cook, stirring with a heatproof spatula, until slightly thickened, about 1 minute. Remove from the heat.

CHILL Gradually whisk the hot milk mixture into the chocolate. Add the salt and whisk until the chocolate is melted and incorporated.

Pour the mixture into a 1-gallon Ziploc freezer bag and submerge the sealed bag in the ice bath. Let stand, adding more ice as necessary, until cold, about 30 minutes.

FREEZE Pour the ice cream base into the frozen canister and spin until thick and creamy.

Pack the ice cream into a storage container, press a sheet of parchment directly against the surface, and seal with an airtight lid. Freeze in the coldest part of your freezer until firm, at least 4 hours.

Milk Chocolate Ice Cream with Sugar-Plumped Raisins

Make and freeze the ice cream. Pack into the storage container, folding in 1½ cups drained Sugar-Plumped Raisins (page 194) as you go.

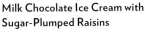

GUCCI MUU MUU

Exotic, sweet curry spices and chocolate are united with rich cream and evaporated milk; toasted coconut throughout gives a chewy texture.

The addition of evaporated milk makes for a wonderful, almost candied, milky ice cream, like Indian kulfi. Even with the worlds of exotic Indian and Thai curries, traditional, easy-to-love yellow curry powder is still at the top of my list. This very popular flavor was inspired by the Indian eatery at the North Market, where I spent my first years making ice creams, and has been in my repertoire since I began playing with these ingredients in 1996. In our shops, it goes by the name Gucci Muu Muu, because the ingredients are a combination of decadent and exotic, and they evoke a colorful pattern.

Pairs well with: Cashews. Sugar-Plumped Golden Raisins (page 194). Bananas.

Makes about 1 quart

1 cup whole milk

1 tablespoon plus 1 teaspoon cornstarch

2 ounces bittersweet chocolate (55% to 70% cocoa)

1 cup evaporated milk

¼ cup heavy cream

⅔ cup sugar

2 tablespoons light corn syrup

⅓ cup unsweetened cocoa powder

1 tablespoon yellow curry powder

½ cup unsweetened shredded coconut. toasted (see page 194)

¼ teaspoon fine sea salt

TASTING NOTES

_____

_____

_____

_____

_____

_____

PREP Mix about 2 tablespoons of the milk with the cornstarch in a small bowl to make a smooth slurry.

Chop the chocolate and put it in a medium bowl.

Fill a large bowl with ice and water.

COOK Combine the remaining milk, the evaporated milk, cream, sugar, and corn syrup in a 4-quart saucepan, and bring to a rolling boil over medium-high heat. Add the cocoa, whisking until incorporated, and continue boiling for 4 minutes.

Remove from the heat and gradually whisk in the cornstarch slurry.

Bring the mixture back to a boil over medium-high heat and cook, stirring with a heatproof spatula, until slightly thickened, about 1 minute. Remove from the heat.

CHILL Gradually whisk the hot milk mixture into the chocolate and stir until the chocolate is melted and incorporated. Add the curry powder, coconut, and salt.

Pour the mixture into a 1-gallon Ziploc freezer bag and submerge the sealed bag in the ice bath. Let stand, adding more ice as necessary, until cold, about 30 minutes.

FREEZE Pour the ice cream base into the frozen canister and spin until thick and creamy.

Pack the ice cream into a storage container, press a sheet of parchment directly against the surface, and seal with an airtight lid. Freeze in the coldest part of your freezer until firm, at least 4 hours.

QUEEN CITY CAYENNE ICE CREAM

Medium-dark chocolate slowly reveals hints of spice. The finish is pleasantly tingly.

This was on my opening menu at my first business, Scream. As soon as I began making it, I understood the enormous potential of ice cream as a host for flavors. I originally called it Mexican Hot Chocolate, until one day it occurred to me that Cincinnati chili—famously made with a hint of chocolate, cinnamon, and cayenne—was a closer-to-home reference. So I renamed it, a nod to our neighbor to the south (and one of our favorite cities), aka "The Queen City."

This is a pleasant medium chocolate, neither super-milky nor super-dark.

Pairs well with: White chocolate. Toasted almonds. Rose water.

Makes about 1 quart

CHOCOLATE PASTE

⅓ cup unsweetened cocoa powder

⅓ cup sugar

⅓ cup water

1½ ounces bittersweet chocolate (55% to 70% cocoa), finely chopped

ICE CREAM BASE

2 cups whole milk

1 tablespoon plus 1 teaspoon cornstarch

1½ ounces (3 tablespoons) cream cheese, softened

⅛ teaspoon fine sea salt

1¼ cups heavy cream

⅔ cup sugar

2 tablespoons light corn syrup

½ teaspoon ground cinnamon

⅛ teaspoon cayenne pepper, or to taste

TASTING NOTES

_____

_____

_____

_____

_____

PREP

For the chocolate paste:

Combine the cocoa, sugar, and water in a small saucepan, bring to a boil over medium heat, stirring to dissolve the sugar, and boil for 30 seconds. Remove from the heat, add the chocolate, and stir until smooth. Set aside.

For the ice cream base:

Mix about 2 tablespoons of the milk with the cornstarch in a small bowl to make a smooth slurry.

Whisk the cream cheese, warm chocolate paste, and salt in a medium bowl until smooth.

Fill a large bowl with ice and water.

COOK Combine the remaining milk, the cream, sugar, and corn syrup in a 4-quart saucepan, bring to a rolling boil over medium-high heat, and boil for 4 minutes. Remove from the heat and gradually whisk in the cornstarch slurry.

Bring the mixture back to a boil over medium-high heat and cook, stirring with a heatproof spatula, until slightly thickened, about 1 minute. Remove from the heat.

CHILL Gradually whisk the hot milk mixture into the cream cheese mixture until smooth. Add the cinnamon and cayenne and stir well.

Pour the mixture into a 1-gallon Ziploc freezer bag and submerge the sealed bag in the ice bath. Let stand, adding more ice as necessary, until cold, about 30 minutes.

FREEZE Pour the ice cream base into the frozen canister and spin until thick and creamy.

Pack the ice cream into a storage container, press a sheet of parchment directly against the surface, and seal with an airtight lid. Freeze in the coldest part of your freezer until firm, at least 4 hours.

BLACK COFFEE ICE CREAM

The aroma of just-roasted coffee is sealed into the cream and then released into your nose as the cream melts on your tongue.

I can't count the number of people who've said, "I am not a coffee drinker, but I *love* the way it smells." There's good reason for this. Our noses detect volatile compounds in the oils of fresh-roasted coffee; when you steep coffee in water, it can taste bitter, and you lose some of the aromatic oils.

For coffee ice cream that tastes as good as coffee smells, we grind just-roasted coffee and add it to warm cream to steep. The butterfat in the cream fuses with the oils in the coffee, and then those flavors are released as the ice cream warms and melts in your mouth.

If you can, buy coffee beans from a local roaster. The flavor is markedly more pronounced when your coffee is superfresh. We have long purchased our coffee from Stauf's Coffee Roasters in Columbus.

Pairs well with: Chocolate freckles (see "Freeze" on page 105). Ugandan Vanilla Bean Ice Cream (page 148) for a café au lait. Salty Caramel Ice Cream (page 102). Whiskey, Bailey's, or Frangelico for a grown-up float.

Makes about 1 quart

2½ cups whole milk

1 tablespoon plus 2 teaspoons cornstarch

1½ ounces (3 tablespoons) cream cheese, softened

⅛ teaspoon fine sea salt

1½ cups heavy cream

¾ cup sugar

3 tablespoons light corn syrup

¼ cup dark-roast coffee beans, coarsely ground

TASTING NOTES

_____

_____

_____

_____

_____

_____

PREP Mix about 2 tablespoons of the milk with the cornstarch in a small bowl to make a smooth slurry.

Whisk the cream cheese and salt in a medium bowl until smooth.

Fill a large bowl with ice and water.

COOK Combine the remaining milk, the cream, sugar, and corn syrup in a 4-quart saucepan, bring to a rolling boil over medium-high heat, and boil for 4 minutes. Remove from the heat, add the coffee, and let steep for 5 minutes.

Strain the milk mixture through a sieve lined with a layer of cheesecloth. Squeeze the coffee in the cheesecloth to extract as much liquid as possible, then discard the grounds.

Return the cream mixture to the saucepan and gradually whisk in the cornstarch slurry. Bring back to a boil over medium-high heat and cook, stirring with a rubber spatula, until slightly thickened, about 1 minute. Remove from the heat.

CHILL Gradually whisk the hot milk mixture into the cream cheese until smooth. Pour the mixture into a 1-gallon Ziploc freezer bag and submerge the sealed bag in the ice bath. Let stand, adding more ice as necessary, until cold, about 30 minutes.

FREEZE Pour the ice cream base into the frozen canister and spin until thick and creamy.

Pack the ice cream into a storage container, press a sheet of parchment directly against the surface, and seal with an airtight lid. Freeze in the coldest part of your freezer until firm, at least 4 hours.

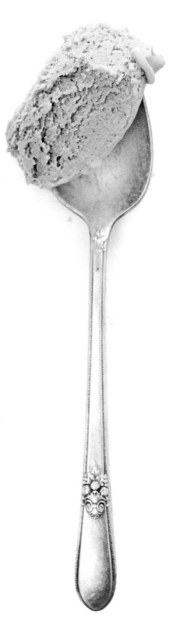

GOOEY BUTTER CAKE ICE CREAM

Honey-Butterscotch-soaked cake and cream cheese ice cream— the scent of a Midwestern kitchen.

Once you've tasted one sugary bite of St. Louis's gooey butter cake, you'll never forget it. It's a famous local specialty, and our ice cream version is as gooey, buttery, and rich as anything I've ever had from a bakery or my mom's kitchen. In our recipe, the ice cream calls for plenty of cream cheese and butter to mimic the "gooey" part of the cake, and the cake pieces have a pleasant firm chewiness.

As in our Savannah Buttermint Ice Cream (page 32), natural butter flavoring is essential for this flavor. It replicates the cake mix–popcorn scent that defines gooey butter cake.

Makes about 1 quart

Half of The Cake (page 197), cut into ½-inch cubes

¾ cup Honey Butterscotch Sauce (page 202)

2 cups whole milk

1 tablespoon plus 1 teaspoon cornstarch

4 ounces (8 tablespoons) cream cheese, softened

½ teaspoon fine sea salt

1¼ cups heavy cream

⅔ cup packed light brown sugar

2 tablespoons light corn syrup

3 to 4 drops Frontier butter flavor (see Sources, page 208)

TASTING NOTES

_____

_____

_____

_____

_____

_____

PREP Put the cake cubes in a large bowl. Toss with the butterscotch sauce and let stand so the cake begins to absorb the sauce.

Mix about 2 tablespoons of the milk with the cornstarch in a small bowl to make a smooth slurry.

Whisk the cream cheese and salt in a medium bowl until smooth.

Fill a large bowl with ice and water.

COOK Combine the remaining milk, the cream, sugar, and corn syrup in a 4-quart saucepan, bring to a rolling boil over medium-high heat, and boil for 4 minutes. Remove from the heat and gradually whisk in the cornstarch slurry.

Bring the mixture back to a boil over medium-high heat and cook, stirring with a heatproof spatula, until slightly thickened, about 1 minute. Remove from the heat.

CHILL Gradually whisk the hot milk mixture into the cream cheese until smooth.

Pour the mixture into a 1-gallon Ziploc freezer bag and submerge the sealed bag in the ice bath. Let stand, adding more ice as necessary, until cold, about 30 minutes.

FREEZE Pour the ice cream base into the frozen canister and turn on the machine. Drop the butter flavoring through the opening in the top of the machine, and continue to spin the ice cream until thick and creamy.

Pack the ice cream into a storage container, layering it with the cake. Press a sheet of parchment directly against the surface, and seal with an airtight lid. Freeze in the coldest part of your freezer until firm, at least 4 hours.

BANGKOK PEANUT ICE CREAM

a complex blend of hot, salty, savory, and sweet.

For years, there was a rivalry in the North Market about who had the best pad Thai. One shop's sign said "Best Pad Thai in the Market," which was answered with another shop's "Best Pad Thai in Columbus." One of the battling merchants was a young Thai woman named Nida. Hers was everything pad Thai should be: fresh and light, exquisitely spiced, and slightly sweet with layers and layers of flavor.

As the debate heated up, I decided to throw my hat in the ring. Using locally produced all-natural peanut butter, ground toasted coconut, and cayenne pepper, I created Bangkok Peanut Ice Cream and, with tongue firmly in cheek, touted it as the "Best Pad Thai in the *World!*"

For more authentic flavor and a lighter finish, add a bruised lemongrass stalk and 4 "coins" of ginger during the boiling stage, then remove before whisking in the cornstarch slurry.

Pairs well with: Lemongrass Dry Soda. Cucumber, Honeydew, & Cayenne Frozen Yogurt (page 78). Praline Sauce (page 201) and bananas.

Makes about 1 quart

1¼ cups whole milk

1 tablespoon plus 2 teaspoons cornstarch

1½ ounces (3 tablespoons) cream cheese, softened

¼ cup natural peanut butter

½ teaspoon fine sea salt

1¼ cups heavy cream

¾ cup unsweetened coconut milk (not light)

⅔ cup sugar

2 tablespoons light corn syrup

2 tablespoons honey

½ cup unsweetened shredded coconut, toasted (see page 194)

⅛ teaspoon cayenne pepper, or to taste

TASTING NOTES

_____

_____

_____

_____

_____

_____

PREP Mix about 2 tablespoons of the milk with the cornstarch in a small bowl to make a smooth slurry.

Whisk the cream cheese, peanut butter, and salt in a medium bowl until smooth.

Fill a large bowl with ice and water.

COOK Combine the remaining milk, the cream, coconut milk, sugar, corn syrup, and honey in a 4-quart saucepan, bring to a rolling boil over medium-high heat, and boil for 4 minutes. Remove from the heat and gradually whisk in the cornstarch slurry.

Bring the mixture back to a boil over medium-high heat and cook, stirring with a heatproof spatula, until slightly thickened, about 1 minute. Remove from the heat.

CHILL Gradually whisk the hot milk mixture into the peanut butter mixture until smooth. Whisk in the toasted coconut and cayenne.

Pour the mixture into a 1-gallon Ziploc freezer bag and submerge the sealed bag in the ice bath. Let stand, adding more ice as necessary, until cold, about 30 minutes.

FREEZE Pour the ice cream base into the frozen canister and spin until thick and creamy.

Pack the ice cream into a storage container, press a sheet of parchment directly against the surface, and seal with an airtight lid. Freeze in the coldest part of your freezer until firm, at least 4 hours.

BLACK WALNUT DIVINITY ICE CREAM

Fragrant black walnuts mellowed by sweet pasture-raised cream.

Ohio black walnuts deserve a place among the world's most prized nuts. The flavors of Piedmont's hazelnuts, Marcona almonds, and pistachios from Sicily and Iran are all wonderful, but they pale in comparison to the piquant Ohio black walnut. Along with sweet corn and black raspberries, black walnuts capture the flavor of Ohio.

Black walnuts pack a lot of nostalgia for me. My grandmother Bette always makes meringue-like black walnut divinity candies, and our Black Walnut Divinity has an old-fashioned flavor profile.

It takes full advantage of the nuts' strong taste. First we toast them, then we grind some of them to a paste. While it is still warm, we mix it into the cream, so the oils in the walnuts adhere to the oils in the butterfat—this locks the walnuts' distinct flavor into the cream. Then, we fold whole toasted black walnuts into the ice cream as it's coming out of the machine.

Makes about 1 quart

1 cup black walnuts

2 cups whole milk

1 tablespoon plus 1 teaspoon cornstarch

1½ ounces (3 tablespoons) cream cheese, softened

¼ teaspoon fine sea salt

1¼ cups heavy cream

⅔ cup sugar

2 tablespoons light corn syrup

TASTING NOTES

PREP Preheat the oven to 350°F.

Spread the walnuts out in one layer on a baking sheet. Toast in the oven until just starting to brown, about 10 minutes. Remove from the oven.

Grind ½ cup of the warm walnuts in the food processor until they become a smooth paste. Reserve the remaining walnuts.

Mix about 2 tablespoons of the milk with the cornstarch in a small bowl to make a smooth slurry.

Whisk the cream cheese, black walnut paste, and salt in a medium bowl until smooth.

Fill a large bowl with ice and water.

COOK Combine the remaining milk, the cream, sugar, and corn syrup in a 4-quart saucepan, bring to a rolling boil over medium-high heat, and boil for 4 minutes. Remove from the heat and gradually whisk in the cornstarch slurry.

Bring the mixture back to a boil over medium-high heat and cook, stirring with a heatproof spatula, until slightly thickened, about 1 minute. Remove from the heat.

CHILL Gradually whisk the hot milk mixture into the cream cheese mixture until smooth.

Pour the mixture into a 1-gallon Ziploc freezer bag and submerge the sealed bag in the ice bath. Let stand, adding more ice as necessary, until cold, about 30 minutes.

FREEZE Pour the ice cream base into the frozen canister and spin until thick and creamy.

Pack the ice cream into a storage container, folding in the remaining black walnuts as you go. Press a sheet of parchment directly against the surface, and seal with an airtight lid. Freeze in the coldest part of your freezer until firm, at least 4 hours.

BROWN BUTTER ALMOND BRITTLE ICE CREAM

Rich brown butter ice cream and salty, crunchy almonds: familiar and delicious.

Krokan is a Norwegian treat made of caramelized butter and almond brittle. When we did a Norway-inspired holiday collection a few years ago, we adapted it into Brown Butter Almond Brittle Ice Cream. It became a best seller and remains on our menu today.

We flavor the ice cream with butter solids, the flavorful bits that fall to the bottom of the pan when butter is heated and separates. When you heat the butter until it just begins to bubble (a few minutes) and separates, you can pour off the butter oil and use the bits at the bottom of the pan to make a wonderful soft-scented butter ice cream. Allow the butter to cook longer, until it turns a rich dark brown (about 10 minutes), and the ice cream will take on a wonderful nuttiness.

Makes about 1 quart

ICE CREAM BASE
2 cups whole milk

1 tablespoon plus 1 teaspoon cornstarch

1½ ounces (3 tablespoons) cream cheese, softened

⅛ teaspoon fine sea salt

¾ pound (3 sticks) unsalted butter

1¼ cups heavy cream

⅔ cup sugar

2 tablespoons light corn syrup

1 cup bite-sized pieces Almond Brittle (page 199), plus larger shreds for garnish (optional)

TASTING NOTES

_____

_____

_____

_____

_____

_____

_____

PREP

Mix about 2 tablespoons of the milk with the cornstarch in a small bowl to make a smooth slurry. Whisk the cream cheese and salt in a medium bowl until smooth. Fill a large bowl with ice and water.

COOK

Melt the butter over medium heat in a 4-quart saucepan. Bring to a boil and let bubble until the foam starts to subside and the butter is a rich dark brown (not black). Remove from the heat and let stand until the butter solids settle to the bottom of the pan, about 5 minutes.

Pour the clear yellow butter oil into a storage container. As you get closer to the butter solids in the bottom of the pan, use a teaspoon to remove as much liquid butter as you can. You should have about 1 tablespoon of brown butter solids and a little bit of melted fat in the bottom of the pan (it is impossible to remove all the melted fat).

Add the remaining milk, the cream, sugar, and corn syrup to the butter solids, bring to a rolling boil over medium-high heat, and boil for 4 minutes. Remove from the heat and gradually whisk in the cornstarch slurry.

Bring the mixture back to a boil over medium-high heat and cook, stirring with a heatproof spatula, until slightly thickened, about 1 minute. Remove from the heat.

CHILL

Gradually whisk the hot milk mixture into the cream cheese mixture until smooth. Pour the mixture into a 1-gallon Ziploc freezer bag and submerge the sealed bag in the ice bath. Let stand, adding more ice as necessary, until cold, about 30 minutes.

FREEZE

Pour the ice cream base into the frozen canister and spin until thick and creamy. Pack the ice cream into a storage container, folding in the chopped almond brittle as you go. Press a sheet of parchment directly against the surface, and seal with an airtight lid. Freeze in the coldest part of your freezer until firm, at least 4 hours.

Butter Ice Cream with Honey Hickory Pralines

Cook the butter for only 5 minutes, until the foam has subsided but the butter has not turned brown: pour off the butter and reserve the solids. Make and spin the ice cream, then pack into the storage container, folding in Honey Hickory Pralines (page 194) as you go.

TOASTED BRIOCHE ICE CREAM WITH BUTTER AND JAM

Butter ice cream with crumbs of toast and a ribbon of fragrant, sweet-tart jam.

The Brown Butter Almond Brittle Ice Cream (page 170) can be customized to make many different flavors. For a collection inspired by Marie Antoinette several years ago, we sprinkled toasted brioche crumbs into the butter base as we removed it from the machine and layered jam into the storage container. *Voilà!*

Toasted Brioche Ice Cream with Butter and Jam, while a play on the brown bread ice creams enjoyed in Ireland, was meant to evoke a Parisian breakfast in the seventeenth century. The following year, it was a part of our Mother's Day collection of flavors inspired by a Parisian breakfast.

Makes about 1 quart

Two 1-inch-thick slices brioche

ICE CREAM BASE

2 cups whole milk

1 tablespoon plus 1 teaspoon cornstarch

1½ ounces (3 tablespoons) cream cheese, softened

⅛ teaspoon fine sea salt

¾ pound (3 sticks) unsalted butter

Raspberry Sauce (page 196) or your favorite jam

1¼ cups heavy cream

⅔ cup sugar

2 tablespoons light corn syrup

TASTING NOTES

_____

_____

_____

_____

_____

_____

ADVANCE PREP Preheat the oven to 250°F.

Toast the brioche (any bread will work) in the oven until completely dry. Grind into fine crumbs. Set aside.

PREP Mix about 2 tablespoons of the milk with the cornstarch in a small bowl to make a smooth slurry.

Whisk the cream cheese and salt in a medium bowl until smooth.

Fill a large bowl with ice and water.

COOK Melt the butter over medium heat in a 4-quart saucepan. Bring to a boil and let bubble until the foam starts to subside and the butter has not yet turned brown. Remove from the heat and let stand until the butter solids settle to the bottom of the pan, about 5 minutes.

Pour the clear yellow butter oil into a storage container. As you get closer to the butter solids in the bottom of the pan, use a teaspoon to remove as much liquid butter as you can. You should have about 1 tablespoon of brown butter solids and a little bit of melted fat in the bottom of the pan (it is impossible to remove all the melted fat).

Add the remaining milk, the cream, sugar, and corn syrup to the butter solids, bring to a rolling boil over medium-high heat, and boil for 4 minutes. Remove from the heat and gradually whisk in the cornstarch slurry.

Bring the mixture back to a boil over medium-high heat and cook, stirring with a heatproof spatula, until slightly thickened, about 1 minute. Remove from the heat.

CHILL Gradually whisk the hot milk mixture into the cream cheese until smooth.

Pour the mixture into a 1-gallon Ziploc freezer bag and submerge the sealed bag in the ice bath. Let stand, adding more ice as necessary, until cold, about 30 minutes.

FREEZE Pour the ice cream base into the frozen canister and turn on the machine. Reserve 2 teaspoons of the bread crumbs. Add the remaining bread crumbs through the opening in the top of the machine, and spin the ice cream until thick and creamy.

Pack the ice cream into the storage container, layering it with Raspberry Sauce or jam and finishing with a spoonful of sauce.

Serve the ice cream sprinkled with the reserved bread crumbs.

TRES LECHES ICE CREAM

Airy morsels of meringue and cubes of buttery cake in a light coconut-milk and cow's-milk ice cream.

What I love about tres leches, the famous cake from Latin America, is the fluffy meringue on top. The cake itself is soaked in three sweetened milks: regular, coconut, and evaporated. The first tres leches cake I ever had was made by a friend of mine from the Dominican Republic. She soaked the not-too-sweet cake in sweetened milk, then topped it with meringue and cherries. It's one of the best desserts I've ever eaten. Sprinkle this with cinnamon to fancy it up for service, or grate palm sugar over the top.

Makes about 1 quart

COCONUT SYRUP

¼ cup unsweetened coconut milk (not light)

2 tablespoons sugar

Half of The Cake (page 197), cut into ½-inch cubes

ICE CREAM BASE

¾ cup whole milk

2 tablespoons cornstarch

1 cup heavy cream

1 cup evaporated milk

½ cup unsweetened coconut milk (not light)

⅔ cup sugar

2 tablespoons light corn syrup

⅛ teaspoon fine sea salt

1 cup crumbled Meringue Shells (page 198: add ½ cup toasted, unsweetened shredded coconut to the recipe if desired), or store-bought meringue

TASTING NOTES

_____

_____

_____

_____

_____

_____

PREP

For the coconut syrup:

Bring the coconut milk and sugar to a boil in a small saucepan, stirring to dissolve the sugar. Remove from the heat.

Put the cake cubes in a bowl. Toss with the coconut milk syrup, and refrigerate.

For the ice cream base:

Mix about 3 tablespoons of the milk with the cornstarch in a small bowl to make a smooth slurry.

Fill a large bowl with ice and water.

COOK Combine the remaining milk, the cream, evaporated milk, coconut milk, sugar, and corn syrup in a 4-quart saucepan, bring to a rolling boil over medium-high heat, and boil for 4 minutes. Remove from the heat and gradually whisk in the cornstarch slurry.

Bring the mixture back to a boil over medium-high heat and cook, stirring with a heatproof spatula, until slightly thickened, about 1 minute. Remove from the heat and add the salt. Let cool for 10 minutes, stirring occasionally.

CHILL Pour the mixture into a 1-gallon Ziploc freezer bag and submerge the sealed bag in the ice bath. Let stand, adding more ice as necessary, until cold, about 30 minutes.

FREEZE Pour the ice cream base into the frozen canister and spin until thick and creamy.

Pack the ice cream into a storage container, layering it with the cubes of coconut cake and meringue as you go; reserve some crumbs and use them to decorate the top. Press a sheet of parchment directly against the surface, and seal with an airtight lid. Freeze in the coldest part of your freezer until firm, at least 4 hours.

LEMON CREAM ICE CREAM

Extra-tart, full-cream lemon, ultra-rich yet light as air; versatile in every season.

This ice cream is really fun. It's very tart and very creamy—two things that don't normally go together. When I eat it, I think of birthdays and baby showers and about how well it would go with all of those tall, round cakes in the window of the local bakery: coconut cake, strawberry with whipped cream and slivered almonds, double chocolate, white cake with lemon curd and raspberry sauce.

Add browned slivered almonds into the ice cream (with sugar-plumped dried cherries; see page 194) to serve after a big Italian meal. It's what you want after you watch the movie *Big Night*. But this ice cream actually came about one year when I wanted something to serve with blackstrap-molasses ginger cake. It excels as a partner to a super-dark ginger cake studded with large pieces of candied ginger.

Other good additions include candied ginger, crushed Lemonheads or other lemon hard candy, and crumbled amaretti. Layer them into the ice cream when you pack it into the freezer container.

Makes about 1 quart

LEMON SYRUP

2 to 3 lemons

2 tablespoons sugar

ICE CREAM BASE

2 cups whole milk

1 tablespoon plus 1 teaspoon cornstarch

1½ ounces (3 tablespoons) cream cheese, softened

⅛ teaspoon fine sea salt

1¼ cups heavy cream

⅔ cup sugar

2 tablespoons light corn syrup

Zest of 2 lemons (reserved from above)

TASTING NOTES

_____

_____

_____

_____

_____

PREP

For the lemon syrup:

Using a vegetable peeler, remove the zest from 2 of the lemons in large strips; reserve. Halve the lemons and squeeze enough juice to make ½ cup.

Combine the lemon juice and sugar in a saucepan and bring to a simmer over medium heat, stirring until the sugar is dissolved. Remove from the heat and refrigerate until chilled.

For the ice cream base:

Mix about 2 tablespoons of the milk with the cornstarch in a small bowl to make a smooth slurry.

Whisk the cream cheese and salt in a medium bowl until smooth.

Fill a large bowl with ice and water.

COOK Combine the remaining milk, the cream, sugar, corn syrup, and lemon zest in a 4-quart saucepan, bring to a rolling boil over medium-high heat, and boil for 4 minutes. Remove from the heat and gradually whisk in the cornstarch slurry.

Bring the mixture back to a boil over medium-high heat and cook, stirring with a heatproof spatula, until slightly thickened, about 1 minute. Remove from the heat.

CHILL Gradually whisk the hot milk mixture into the cream cheese until smooth.

Pour the mixture into a 1-gallon Ziploc freezer bag and submerge the sealed bag in the ice bath. Let stand, adding more ice as necessary, until cold, about 30 minutes.

FREEZE Remove the lemon zest. Pour the ice cream base into the frozen canister and turn on the machine. Pour the lemon syrup through the opening in the top of the machine, and continue to spin the ice cream until thick and creamy.

Pack the ice cream into a storage container, press a sheet of parchment directly against the surface, and seal with an airtight lid. Freeze in the coldest part of your freezer until firm, at least 4 hours.

GRAPEFRUIT HIBISCUS FROZEN YOGURT

Slightly bitter grapefruit flavors this distinctively refreshing frozen yogurt; hibiscus has a pleasant, earthy taste with notes of cranberry.

Grapefruit yogurt is one of my favorite flavors. We often make this at the end of winter, when local fruits are not available but people are beginning to crave the lighter flavors of spring. It's pretty and cheerful, and it makes a great late-winter offering.

Pairs well with: Champagne. Gingersnaps. Chocolate.

Makes a generous 1 quart

FROZEN YOGURT BASE

1 quart plain low-fat yogurt

1½ cups whole milk

2 tablespoons cornstarch

2 ounces (4 tablespoons) cream cheese, softened

½ cup heavy cream

⅔ cup sugar

¼ cup light corn syrup

Zest of 1 grapefruit (reserved)

GRAPEFRUIT SYRUP

1 grapefruit

2 tablespoons sugar

¼ cup dried hibiscus (see Sources, page 208)

TASTING NOTES

ADVANCE PREP

For the strained yogurt:

Fit a sieve over a bowl and line it with two layers of cheesecloth. Pour the yogurt into the lined sieve, cover with plastic wrap, and refrigerate for 6 to 8 hours to drain. Discard the liquid, and measure out 1¼ cups of the strained yogurt; set aside.

For the grapefruit syrup:

Using a vegetable peeler, remove the zest from the grapefruit in large strips; set aside. Halve the grapefruit and squeeze enough juice to measure ½ cup. Combine the grapefruit juice and sugar in a small saucepan and bring to a boil over medium-high heat, stirring to dissolve the sugar. Remove from the heat, add the hibiscus flowers, and let steep for 10 minutes.

Strain the syrup through a sieve, pressing on the flowers to release as much liquid as possible.

PREP Mix about 3 tablespoons of the milk with the cornstarch in a small bowl to make a smooth slurry.

Whisk the cream cheese in a medium bowl until smooth.

Fill a large bowl with ice and water.

COOK Combine the remaining milk, the cream, sugar, corn syrup, and grapefruit zest in a 4-quart saucepan, bring to a rolling boil over medium-high heat, and boil for 4 minutes. Remove from the heat and gradually whisk in the cornstarch slurry.

Bring the mixture back to a boil over medium-high heat and cook, stirring with a heatproof spatula, until slightly thickened, about 1 minute. Remove from the heat.

CHILL Gradually whisk the hot milk mixture into the cream cheese until smooth. Add the 1¼ cups yogurt and the grapefruit syrup and whisk until smooth.

Pour the mixture into a 1-gallon Ziploc freezer bag and submerge the sealed bag in the ice bath. Let stand, adding more ice as necessary, until cold, about 30 minutes.

FREEZE Remove the zest. Pour the frozen yogurt base into the frozen canister and spin until thick and creamy.

Pack the frozen yogurt into a storage container, press a sheet of parchment directly against the surface, and seal with an airtight lid. Freeze in the coldest part of your freezer until firm, at least 4 hours.

INFLUENZA RX SORBET

Our flu-season fix: proven to clear nasal passages, ease a sore throat, and soothe the body.

Whenever there's a really severe flu season, we make this good-for-what-ails-you sorbet, modeled on the home remedy my mother and grandmother made when anyone in the family was under the weather. Sniffles, aches, and fevers meant one thing: a mug of hot whiskey with honey and lemon juice, then straight to bed.

That remedy is equally soothing as a cold sorbet. Each ingredient has natural healing properties. Lemon and orange juice have plenty of vitamin C. Ginger and cayenne clear nasal passages and have antiseptic properties. Powerful humectants, honey and liquid pectin help a dry, itchy throat retain moisture. Honey also has antiseptic qualities, as does bourbon. And a frozen sorbet calms an inflamed sore throat.

In our shops, we tend to keep pints of these sorbets at the bottom of our freezers. If we catch someone sniffling or if a customer mentions a sick little one at home, we send them home with a pint.

Pairs well with: A box of tissues and a bed made up on the couch.

Makes a generous 1 quart

2 cups fresh orange juice
(from 5 to 6 oranges)

⅓ cup fresh lemon juice
(from about 2 lemons)

⅔ cup sugar

⅓ cup honey

¼ teaspoon powdered ginger

One 3-ounce packet liquid pectin

⅛ teaspoon cayenne

2 to 4 tablespoons Maker's Mark
bourbon (optional)

TASTING NOTES

_____

_____

_____

_____

_____

_____

COOK Combine the orange and lemon juices, sugar, honey, and ginger in a medium saucepan and bring to a boil, stirring to dissolve the sugar. Remove from the heat.

CHILL Add the pectin, cayenne, and bourbon, if using. Pour into a bowl, cover, and refrigerate until cold.

FREEZE Freeze the sorbet just until it is the consistency of very softly whipped cream. (You can eat it now, if you wish; otherwise, proceed as directed.)

Pack the sorbet into a storage container, press a sheet of parchment directly against the surface, and seal with an airtight lid. Freeze in the coldest part of your freezer until firm, at least 4 hours.

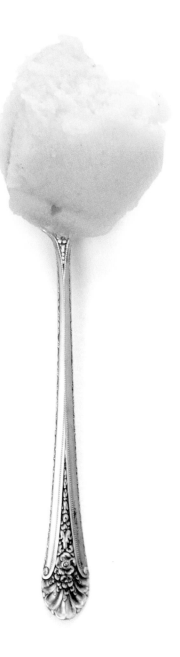

generous
cinnamon Sugar
sprinkle coating

wedge of
Chocolate
Frito Crunch

¼ cup of
Praline
Sauce

Makes 6 servings

CHOCOLATE FRITO CRUNCH
8 ounces bittersweet chocolate, chopped

2 tablespoons ground Fritos

CINNAMON SUGAR
¼ cup turbinado sugar

2 teaspoons ground cinnamon, preferably Vietnamese

Queen City Cayenne Ice Cream (page 160)
1½ cups **Praline Sauce (page 201)**, warmed
Whipped Cream (page 203)
Salty Buttered Almonds (page 194) (optional)

For the chocolate crunch:
Line a baking sheet with a Silpat or parchment. Melt
the chocolate in a double boiler. Add the Fritos and
spread in a thin layer on the baking sheet. Let cool
completely (or freeze). Break up into 6 or more
wedges.

For the cinnamon sugar:
Blend the sugar and cinnamon together.

To assemble the sundaes:
Place 2 small scoops of ice cream on each plate
(or assemble the sundaes in wide-mouthed Mason
jars). Top each with ¼ cup praline sauce and a large
dollop of whipped cream. Sprinkle cinnamon sugar
generously over the whipped cream and scatter the
almonds, if using, over the sundaes. Garnish each with
a wedge of chocolate crunch.

1 big
scoop of
Queen City Cayenne

CHOCOMOLE SUNDAE

For years, Tapatio was one of the best restaurants in Columbus. Owned by Bruce Hildreth, a chef and very good friend and mentor to me, it was across from the North Market. I often asked Bruce for advice and would sit at his bar after work eating, drinking, and making new friends. Cancer took him a few years ago, and we still miss him and his amazing restaurant. Nothing can compare to Bruce's guava and Brie quesadillas, blue corn cakes with shrimp and cayenne beurre blanc, and beyond-amazing margaritas.

One day near the end of his life, Bruce came to see me at the North Market. He said he had something to give me. He had already given me so much: his recipes for brownies and gazpacho, equipment from his restaurant, and countless hours of advice over the years. This gift was one word: *chocomole*. It was a name for a flavor of ice cream or a sundae or whatever I wanted to do with it. I didn't know what the flavor would be, but I promised him I would make something of it and think of him whenever I did. It had to be something special—Bruce was a celebration: it had to be a sundae.

Bruce—this one is for you.

a dollop of Whipped Cream

cone
Fortune
Cookie

Makes 6 servings

6 bananas, sliced lengthwise in half

Bangkok Peanut Ice Cream
(page 166)

1½ cups Praline Sauce (page 201), warmed

Whipped Cream (page 203)

About ¾ cup Spanish peanuts

6 Fortune Cookies (page 203)

1 basil sprig or 6 cilantro sprigs (optional)

1 large scoop of
Bangkok Peanut

To assemble the sundaes:
Lay 1 halved banana on each plate or large
bowl and place 2 small scoops of ice cream
on top. Top with ¼ cup of the sauce, a large
dollop of whipped cream, and a scattering of
peanuts. Set a fortune cookie to the side of the
sundae and garnish the whipped cream with
the basil or the cilantro sprigs, if using.

2 large dollops of
Whipped Cream

ONE NIGHT IN BANGKOK SUNDAE

This sundae is familiar like a candy bar, sweet, salty, ooey-gooey. The banana underneath the peanut butter coconut milk ice cream takes it over the top in a King-of-Rock-'n'-Roll-meets-The-King-of-Siam kind of way. When I was pregnant with Greta, and then with Dashiell, I ate a couple of these a week. This sundae offers an intensely craveable synergy of flavors and textures.

¼ cup
Praline Sauce

several spoonfuls
of Spanish peanuts

BAKED ALASKA PIE

We send our little scooter truck loaded with tiny Baked Alaska Pies to fancy parties. When the driver fires up a blowtorch and torches the meringue right there, it borders on performance art. Each of those little pies serves 2 people, but here I give the ultimate party recipe for one large pie that serves 8. These pies are so tasty we can't stop eating them. And they are beautiful. The Italian meringue is voluptuous and velvety in your mouth—like the inside of a campfire marshmallow.

The dessert is versatile, too. With Sweet Potato Ice Cream (page 126), it takes on a Thanksgiving personality. With dark chocolate, coconut, banana, or lemon ice cream, it feels like dessert à la Route 66: chocolate silk, coconut cream, banana cream, or lemon meringue pies. With Roasted Strawberry & Buttermilk Ice Cream (page 30), made with the addition of a teaspoon of rose water or a drop of essential oil, if you like, it becomes an elegant spring offering. And if the pie is impressive with one flavor, it is mindblowingly gorgeous and yummy when made with half ice cream and half sorbet layered together. You could even add a thin layer of our Extra-Bitter Hot Fudge Sauce (page 201) or any other sauce in the book atop the ice cream before topping it with the meringue. It's yours to create.

Though Italian meringue is slightly more work than the simpler French meringue in the recipe on page 198, the result is silky and billowy and worth the extra bit of effort.

For the pie crust:

Combine the all-purpose flour, whole wheat flour, and oats in a food processor and process until the oats are in bits. Add the sugar and salt and pulse to combine. Add the butter and pulse just until the dough begins to come together and looks crumbly.

Whisk the egg yolk and half-and-half together in a small bowl. Add the vanilla and whisk to combine. Add to the flour mixture and pulse until the mixture forms a dough.

Turn the dough out onto a lightly floured surface, gather it into a ball, and press into a disk. Wrap in plastic and refrigerate until firm, about 1 hour.

Remove the dough from the refrigerator and let warm for a few minutes to relax the dough. On a lightly floured surface, roll the dough into a circle just under ¼ inch thick.

Gently fold the circle over the rolling pin and lift into a 9-inch pie pan. Press the dough into the pan and trim the edges to a ½-inch overhang. Roll the edge of the dough under itself and tuck and pinch to create a fluted edge; you can also use a fork to create a decorative finish. Refrigerate for 30 minutes.

Preheat the oven to 350°F.

Prick the bottom of the dough all over with a fork. Line with a square of parchment paper and fill with pie weights or dried beans. Bake for 12 minutes.

Lift out the liner and weights and bake for another 12 to 15 minutes, or until the shell is lightly browned and cooked through on the bottom. Let cool, then wrap well in plastic wrap and freeze. Fill the shell with the ice cream, cover with plastic wrap, and freeze for at least 4 hours.

For the meringue:

Put the egg whites in the bowl of a stand mixer fitted with a whisk attachment. Combine the sugar, water, corn syrup, and salt in a heavy-bottomed saucepan and bring to a boil over medium-high heat, stirring once or twice to dissolve the sugar; once the sugar is dissolved, do not stir the syrup again. Insert a candy thermometer in the pan.

When the syrup reaches 215°F, turn the mixer on to medium speed and start whipping the egg whites. (You want to time the whipping of the egg whites so that they reach soft peaks by the time the syrup is ready.) When the egg whites begin to foam, add the cream of tartar.

When the syrup reaches 238°F, remove it from the heat. With the mixer on medium speed, carefully pour the syrup out in a slow, steady stream down the side of the mixer bowl—be careful not to let the stream of syrup come into contact with the whisk. Once all of the syrup has been added, add the vanilla seeds, if using, turn the speed up

Serves 8

PIE CRUST

¾ cup all-purpose flour

¼ cup whole wheat flour

½ cup old-fashioned oats

2 tablespoons light brown sugar

¼ teaspoon fine sea salt

8 tablespoons (1 stick) unsalted butter, cut into ½-inch cubes and chilled

1 large egg yolk

2 tablespoons half-and-half

¼ teaspoon vanilla extract

1 batch ice cream or sorbet of your choice, slightly softened if necessary

ITALIAN MERINGUE

4 large egg whites

1 cup granulated sugar

¼ cup water

1 tablespoon light corn syrup

Pinch of fine sea salt

Pinch of cream of tartar

1 vanilla bean, split, seeds scraped out and reserved (optional)

TASTING NOTES

_____

_____

_____

_____

_____

_____

to high, and whip until the meringue forms billowy peaks and is cool.

Remove the ice cream pie from the freezer and mound dollops of the meringue on top. Place in the freezer, uncovered, until ready to serve. (The assembled pie can be stored in your freezer for up to a month. Once the meringue has frozen, wrap the entire pie in plastic wrap.)

Preheat the oven to 475°F. Remove the pie from the freezer and bake for about 5 minutes, just enough to brown the meringue on top and slightly melt the edges of the ice cream. Slice and serve.

THE BASICS

The following pages contain recipes and techniques we use to customize ice cream ingredients. Don't be afraid to pull ideas from throughout this book, tweak them, and combine them with any other element from this book or elsewhere. You can't go wrong with chopped candies or roasted nuts. Almost any baked good is excellent when chunked into ice cream. And just about any fruit can be roasted—or made into a sauce, as I outline here. Any nut can be turned into pralines; and any dried fruit can be plumped with any sugar or spirit.

● ● ● ● ●

BASES & TECHNIQUES

● ○ ● ● ● ● ○ ○ ● ●

ICE CREAM BASE

Your go-to recipe for experimenting

Makes about 1 quart

2 cups whole milk

1 tablespoon plus 1 teaspoon cornstarch

1½ ounces (3 tablespoons) cream cheese, softened

⅛ teaspoon fine sea salt

1¼ cups heavy cream

⅔ cup sugar

2 tablespoons light corn syrup

PREP Mix about 2 tablespoons of the milk with the cornstarch in a small bowl to make a smooth slurry.

Whisk the cream cheese and salt in a medium bowl until smooth.

Fill a large bowl with ice and water.

COOK Combine the remaining milk, the cream, sugar, and corn syrup in a 4-quart saucepan, bring to a rolling boil over medium-high heat, and boil for 4 minutes. Remove from the heat and gradually whisk in the cornstarch slurry.

Return the mixture to a boil over medium-high heat and cook, stirring until the mixture is slightly thickened, about 1 minute. Remove from the heat.

CHILL Gradually whisk the hot milk mixture into the cream cheese until smooth.

Pour the mixture into a 1-gallon Ziploc freezer bag and submerge the sealed bag in the ice bath. Let stand, adding more ice as necessary, until cold, about 30 minutes.

FREEZE Pour the ice cream base into the frozen canister and spin until thick and creamy.

Pack the ice cream into a storage container, press a sheet of parchment directly against the surface, and seal with an airtight lid. Freeze in the coldest part of your freezer until firm, at least 4 hours.

● ○ ● ● ● ● ○ ● ● ●

FROZEN YOGURT BASE

Makes about 1 quart

1 quart plain low-fat yogurt

1½ cups whole milk

2 tablespoons cornstarch

2 ounces (4 tablespoons) cream cheese, softened

½ cup heavy cream

⅔ cup sugar

¼ cup light corn syrup

ADVANCE PREP Fit a sieve over a bowl and line it with two layers of cheesecloth. Pour the yogurt into the lined sieve, cover with plastic wrap, and refrigerate for 6 to 8 hours to drain. Discard the liquid, and measure out 1¼ cups of the strained yogurt; set aside.

PREP Mix about 3 tablespoons of the milk with the cornstarch in a small bowl to make a smooth slurry.

Whisk the cream cheese in a medium bowl until smooth.

Fill a large bowl with ice and water.

COOK Combine the remaining milk, the cream, sugar, and corn syrup in a 4-quart saucepan, bring to a rolling boil over medium-high heat, and boil for 4 minutes. Remove from the heat and gradually whisk in the cornstarch mixture.

Return the mixture to a boil over medium-high heat and cook, stirring until slightly thickened, about 1 minute. Remove from the heat.

CHILL Gradually whisk the hot milk mixture into the cream cheese until smooth. Add the 1¼ cups yogurt and blend well.

Pour the mixture into a 1-gallon Ziploc freezer bag and submerge the sealed bag in the ice bath. Let stand, adding more ice as necessary, until cold, about 30 minutes.

FREEZE Pour the frozen yogurt base into the frozen canister and spin until thick and creamy.

Pack the frozen yogurt into a storage container, press a sheet of parchment directly against the surface, and seal with an airtight lid. Freeze in the coldest part of your freezer until firm, at least 4 hours.

HOW TO
HOMOGENIZE

If you are using nonhomogenized milk and cream, you will need to take an extra step to fully homogenize the mixture. Otherwise, the butterfat will clump together in the churning process and your ice cream will be buttery and grainy.

As the mixture is heating, prepare an ice bath. After the mixture is heated, pour the hot ice cream base into a food processor, process for 2 minutes, and then chill it in the ice bath. Just before you pour the base into the ice cream machine, return the base to the food processor for another 2 minutes.

NUTS & DRIED FRUITS

HONEY NUT PRALINES

These shellacked nuts begin to melt in the ice cream, creating wonderful pockets of sauce. They are your go-to praline for ice cream. Add as many or as few as you like to any flavor (or just to sweet cream). You can spice them up with a pinch of cayenne (a favorite winter flavor in our shops). Or follow the variation for a stronger flavor.

Makes about 1 cup

1 cup pine nuts, walnuts, black walnuts, or pecans, halved if you prefer smaller bits
2 tablespoons light brown sugar
2 tablespoons honey
1 tablespoon unsalted butter, melted
¼ teaspoon fine sea salt

Preheat the oven to 350°F.

Combine the nuts with the remaining ingredients in a bowl, tossing to coat. Spread out on a baking sheet and bake for 8 minutes. Stir and bake for another 5 to 6 minutes, stirring twice; the nuts should look bubbly and somewhat dry. Remove from the oven and let cool completely, stirring the nuts every couple of minutes to break them up.

VARIATION
Blackstrap Pralines
Substitute blackstrap molasses for the honey and add ¼ teaspoon ground cinnamon to the nut mixture.

SALTY BUTTERED NUTS

Properly toasted almonds, pecans, walnuts, hickory nuts, and other nuts have lots of flavor and just the right amount of salt to pop through the sweet cream. Because flavors are dampened when the ice cream is frozen, I always make sure that these are quite salty. I think it's a nice contrast to the cream. You can use any nut and you will know it's finished toasting when the aroma begins to fill your kitchen. Keep your eye on them or they will burn quickly—especially when preparing smaller varieties like pine nuts.

Makes ¾ cup

¾ cup nut halves or quarters
1 tablespoon unsalted butter, melted
½ teaspoon fine sea salt

Preheat the oven to 350°F.

Combine the nuts with the butter and salt in a bowl, tossing to coat. Spread evenly on a baking sheet and bake for 10 to 15 minutes, turning once, until crisp and aromatic. Let cool completely.

TOASTED COCONUT

Our Bangkok Peanut Ice Cream (page 166) is not the same without evenly toasted coconut. It's essential for flavor here that you use unsweetened coconut and toast it until nicely browned.

Makes 1 cup

1 cup unsweetened shredded coconut

Preheat the oven to 325°F.

Spread the coconut on a baking sheet and toast in the oven, turning and stirring every few minutes, until evenly browned, about 7 minutes. Watch carefully, as coconut can burn quickly. Remove from the oven and let cool.

SUGAR-PLUMPED FRUITS

The beauty of the sugar-plumped fruit is that the fruit remains soft in the ice cream. It's another way to layer in flavor and texture—feel free to use more or less as you like.

Makes about 1 cup strained fruit or 1½ cups sauce

1 cup dried fruit, such as apricots, cherries, cranberries, raisins, prunes, and/or figs (larger fruits chopped into ½-inch pieces)
½ cup plus 1 tablespoon water
½ cup sugar

Put the fruit in a heatproof bowl.

Combine the water and sugar in a small saucepan and bring to a boil, stirring to dissolve the sugar. Pour the syrup over the fruit and let cool to room temperature. Refrigerate until chilled (the fruit will keep for up to a month in the refrigerator).

TWO WAYS TO USE THE FRUIT

Sugar-Plumped Fruits and Liquor-Plumped Fruits can be used in my recipes in one of these two ways.
• As a chunky fruit mix-in: Drain the fruit and discard the syrup.
• As a fruit sauce: Drain the fruit, reserving the syrup. Puree all or half of the fruit in a food processor, adding the syrup as needed until the mixture has the consistency of a sauce. Combine with the remaining fruit, if you didn't puree it all.

LIQUOR-PLUMPED FRUITS

Always stick to my recipes as far as the amount of alcohol is concerned, but decide for yourself how much liquor-plumped fruit you want to add to the ice creams. When it comes to spirited fruits, as with candied fruits, sometimes less is more. For instance, vodka cuts through the cream and offers an invigorating bite. Rum infuses raisins beautifully and leaves notes of caramel on the nose. But keep in mind that you have your own tastes and I have mine. Sometimes I want only an occasional encounter with a fruit, and sometimes I want it in every bite. So how much you add is entirely up to you.

Makes about 1 cup strained fruit or 1½ cups sauce

1 cup dried fruit, such as apricots, cherries, cranberries, currants, raisins, prunes, and/or figs (larger fruits cut into ½-inch pieces)

½ cup water

2 tablespoons rum, grappa, vodka, tequila, bourbon, or liqueur

½ cup sugar

Put the fruit in a heatproof bowl.

Combine the water, rum, and sugar in a small saucepan and bring to a boil, stirring to dissolve the sugar. Pour the syrup over the fruit and let cool to room temperature. Refrigerate until chilled (the fruit will keep for up to a month in the refrigerator).

● ○ ● ○ ● ● ○ ○ ● ●

PLUM PUDDING FRUITS

Versatile for holiday ice creams, these are citrusy, boozy, and aromatic fruits, and they are great when combined with Blackstrap Praline Ice Cream (page 116), Lemon Cream Ice Cream (page 176), and Cognac Ice Cream (page 112) or either of its variations.

Makes 1 cup

¾ cup diced prunes, dried currants, and raisins (any combination)

½ cup sugar

¼ cup water

2 tablespoons Cognac or other brandy

2 tablespoons fresh lemon juice

2 tablespoons finely diced candied ginger

Very finely grated zest of 1 lemon

Combine all the ingredients in a medium saucepan and bring to a boil. Remove from the heat, let cool, and refrigerate. Drain the fruits before using.

● ○ ● ● ● ● ○ ● ○ ●

COGNAC FIG SAUCE

This is a great sauce for any cheese ice cream.

Makes about 1½ cups

1 cup dried figs, coarsely chopped

½ cup honey

½ cup water

¼ cup Cognac

Combine the figs, honey, and water in a small saucepan, bring to a simmer, and simmer for 5 minutes. Remove from the heat; let cool.

Drain the figs, reserving the syrup. Puree half of the figs in a food processor and then add Cognac and enough of the reserved syrup, a little at a time, to thin the puree into a loose paste. Combine the pureed figs with the chopped figs and chill thoroughly.

VARIEGATES & FRUITS FOR ICE CREAMS

ROASTED CHERRIES

Roasting cherries concentrates the flavors and natural fruit sugars. Roasted cherries are great for putting in ice cream, for adding on top of it while serving, or even in a pie à la mode sundae (see page 50).

Makes about 1¼ cups

2 cups pitted fresh or frozen (not thawed) red or black cherries

⅔ cup sugar

2 teaspoons cornstarch

Preheat the oven to 400°F.

Combine the cherries, sugar, and cornstarch in a 9-inch square baking dish, tossing to mix. Roast for 30 to 45 minutes, until the juices are thickened and bubbly, stirring every 15 minutes. Let cool completely, then chill in the refrigerator.

BRANDIED CHERRIES

Great atop any of our sundaes. Or serve the cherries as a sauce.

Makes 3½ cups

1 pound fresh black cherries, pitted, or frozen black cherries

¼ cup sugar

¼ cup brandy

Combine the cherries, sugar, and brandy in a medium saucepan and bring to a boil, stirring to dissolve the sugar. Boil for 5 minutes, then remove from the heat and let cool. Refrigerate, overnight if possible, before serving.

BLUEBERRY SAUCE

Fabulous with citrus yogurts or in sundaes, this sauce is versatile, easy, and gorgeous.

Makes about 1¾ cups

1½ cups blueberries

¾ cup sugar

Mix the blueberries and sugar in a small saucepan and bring to a boil over medium heat. Reduce the heat and simmer, stirring occasionally, until the berries are tender and the sauce is thickened,

about 8 minutes. Remove from the heat and let cool, then refrigerate until cold before using.

RASPBERRY, BLACK RASPBERRY, OR BLACKBERRY SAUCE

This sauce will not freeze fully when it's frozen, so it's perfect to swirl through any ice cream.

Makes about 1¼ cups

2 cups raspberries, black raspberries, and/or blackberries

1 cup sugar

Combine the berries and sugar in a small saucepan and bring to a boil over medium-high heat. Continue boiling, stirring occasionally, until it reaches 220°F (5 to 8 minutes). Let cool slightly, then force through a sieve to remove the seeds. (Or leave a few seeds in there just to prove you made it.) Refrigerate until cold before using.

BAKED GOODS & CANDIES

● ○ ● ○ ● ○ ● ○ ● ○ ● ●

VANILLA BEAN MARSHMALLOWS

Don't ask me how two simple ingredients—sugar and gelatin—can make such a legendary treat. We make our marshmallows with vanilla beans and a pinch of salt to save them from the land of teeth-shattering sweetness. But they are still heavenly even if you leave out the vanilla. Tucked inside of Roxbury Road Ice Cream (page 156), if given a week, they will begin to melt. Fortunately, the ice cream will still be of equal quality a week after it's made, because those partially melted marshmallows are something you may want to wait for. Or torch the entire pan for roasted marshmallows; let cool before cutting. Stuff those burnt mallows into Sweet Potato Ice Cream (page 126), or make your own s'mores ice cream with chocolate, graham crackers, and these marshmallows.

The recipe makes enough for two batches of ice cream; don't be tempted to halve it, because it won't fluff up properly. But the marshmallows will keep for up to 2 weeks, and I'm sure you will find a way to get through any extras. We use them to make Rice Krispie treats for team lunches, and of course, they cannot be beat when added to hot chocolate. In the winter, Charly and I steal some marshmallows from the kitchen, cut to the exact right size, and, with Greta and Dash, make s'mores at home in our fireplace, with Askinosie chocolate.

Makes about 4 cups ½-inch marshmallows

½ cup cold water
Three ¼-ounce packets gelatin
2 cups sugar
¾ cup corn syrup
¼ teaspoon fine sea salt
1 vanilla bean, split, seeds scraped out and reserved
Confectioners' sugar for dusting

Grease a baking sheet with vegetable oil. Line with parchment paper and generously grease the paper. Put ¼ cup of the water in the bowl of a stand mixer fitted with the whisk attachment and sprinkle the gelatin over it. Let it soften for 5 minutes.

Meanwhile, combine the remaining ¼ cup water, the sugar, corn syrup, salt, and vanilla seeds in a medium saucepan and bring to a boil, stirring to dissolve the sugar. Insert a candy thermometer in the pan and cook, without stirring, until the syrup reaches 236°F.

Turn the mixer onto low speed and mix to break up the gelatin. With the mixer running, slowly drizzle the hot syrup into the gelatin, taking care to avoid the spinning whisk. Turn the mixer up to medium and then to high and continue beating until the mixture is very frothy, thick, and cool, about 12 minutes.

Turn the mixture out onto the greased pan. Wet your hands and smooth and spread the marshmallows out in the pan. Cover with a sheet of well-greased plastic wrap or parchment and let stand overnight.

Cut the marshmallows into ½-inch cubes and toss with powdered sugar to coat.

● ○ ● ○ ● ● ○ ○ ● ●

THE CAKE

A good all-purpose cake for mixing into ice cream, because it holds its shape and absorbs sugar syrup. It's a simple cake that adds texture and flavor to ice cream. It can be flavored with cinnamon (¼ to ½ teaspoon) or other spices, depending on the ice cream you choose.

This cake is also what we use to make biscotti to garnish our Tuscan Sundae (page 139) or to

SUNDAE ACCESSORIES

we roll the chocolate-coated ice cream quickly in chopped nuts or pretzels before the chocolate hardens. The chocolate can also be layered into just-churned ice cream to make large melt-in-your-mouth chocolate chunks; see the third variation.

Makes enough to coat 6 to 8 scoops

12 ounces bittersweet chocolate (60% or greater cocoa), chopped

⅓ cup coconut oil

Combine the chocolate and coconut oil in a double boiler and heat, stirring frequently, until the chocolate is almost melted. Remove from the heat and stir until completely melted and smooth. Let cool, then store, covered or in a jar, in the refrigerator. The chocolate will keep for up to 3 weeks.

To use the chocolate, you can melt it just by leaving it in a warm place—like a windowsill or the porch—for half an hour or so, then stir until smooth. Or scrape it into a bowl, set it in a larger bowl of very warm tap water, and let stand, stirring occasionally, until liquefied and smooth. You can also melt it in the microwave, heating it for 20-second intervals and stirring often, but be careful not to let it overheat.

VARIATIONS

Chocolate Orange Shell Add 2 to 3 drops orange essential oil (see Sources, page 208) to the melted chocolate mixture.

White Chocolate Shell Substitute high-quality white chocolate for the bittersweet chocolate.

Chocolate Chunks The chocolate can be poured into the just-churned ice cream. To make large chunks of chocolate chips that melt perfectly when you bite into them, use half the recipe and make sure the chocolate is cool, but still pourable. Layer the ice cream into the storage container with spoonfuls of the liquid chocolate, then freeze until firm.

CARAMELIZED WHITE CHOCOLATE BOMBE SHELL

Caramelized white chocolate is high impact but very easy to make. The refined coconut oil makes it brittle when frozen, yet pourable for adding to machines or coating cones. When adding this to ice cream to make "freckles," you only need to use half of this recipe, but I suggest making the whole thing because the recipe works better with these amounts. And it will last for a month in your refrigerator. I love these freckles in our Banana Ice Cream (page 152).

Makes enough to coat 6 to 8 scoops

12 ounces white chocolate, chopped

½ cup refined coconut oil

Combine the white chocolate and coconut oil in a saucepan

CHOCOLATE BOMBE SHELL

This chocolate is liquid at room temperature but it forms a very brittle shell when poured onto ice cream. The secret is the coconut oil, which is liquid at 76°F and warmer but brittle when cold. I prefer the unrefined version, which has a pronounced coconut flavor. If you are not a coconut lover, you can also find refined coconut oil, which does not taste like coconut.

If you like, add 3 tablespoons of cornflake "dust" to the liquid chocolate for flavor and crunchiness as you chew. When we use this for dipping cones, and cook over medium-low heat, stirring, until melted and smooth. Then continue to cook, stirring constantly, until the mixture becomes a lovely deep amber, for 12 to 15 minutes. Continue to stir constantly, or the chocolate will burn as the color deepens. Remove from the heat if it seems the chocolate is caramelizing too rapidly.

You may take the caramelization further if you wish or do less, depending on your taste. Let cool, then store, covered or in a jar, in the refrigerator. The caramelized chocolate will keep for up to 1 month.

To melt the white chocolate, scrape it into a bowl, set it in a larger bowl of hot tap water, and let stand, stirring occasionally, just until liquefied and smooth.

● ● ● ● ● ● ● ● ● ● ●

RED RASPBERRY-LINGONBERRY SAUCE FOR SUNDAES

This is a brilliant red sauce, perfect on our Oslo Ambrosia sundae (page 136) or any ice cream. More and more stores are beginning to carry lingonberry preserves, but if you can't find them, it's okay to omit them—the sauce and sundae will be delicious even without them!

Makes about 1½ cups

1 cup sugar

One 10-ounce bag frozen raspberries, or 1 pint fresh

½ cup lingonberry preserves

Sprinkle the sugar over the raspberries in a bowl. Let macerate for 2 hours in the refrigerator. Stir in the lingonberry preserves.

● ● ● ● ● ● ● ● ● ● ●

PRALINE SAUCE

This sauce tastes like the buttery brown sugar candy that enrobes the pecans in a New Orleans praline. In our kitchen, we make this with dark muscovado sugar, which is sugar that has not had the molasses removed. It's really nice. You can get the same flavor by using half dark and half light brown sugar. This sauce has a 7-day shelf life—because of the high sugar content, it will start to crystallize after that. Served over Ugandan Vanilla Bean (page 148) or Bangkok Peanut Ice Cream (page 166), it will knock your socks off!

The sauce will separate when cool, because it has a lot of sugar, but just heat it over medium-low heat, stirring, and it will come back together.

Makes about 3 cups

2 cups heavy cream

2 cups packed muscovado sugar or 1 cup each packed dark brown and light brown sugar

½ vanilla bean, split, seeds scraped out, seeds and bean reserved

¼ teaspoon fine sea salt

1 teaspoon vanilla extract

Combine the cream, sugar, vanilla seeds and bean, and the salt in a heavy-bottomed saucepan, bring

to a boil over medium-high heat, stirring to dissolve the sugar, and boil for 7 minutes, or until the sauce thickens a bit. Remove from the heat and add the vanilla extract. Serve warm, or let cool and refrigerate. The sauce will keep for up to 1 week.

To serve, reheat, stirring, until the sauce is warm and fluid.

● ● ● ● ● ● ● ● ● ● ●

EXTRA-BITTER HOT FUDGE SAUCE

The hot fudge you make with this recipe will be the best you've ever tasted. You'll notice that there is no cream in it, as there is in some hot fudge sauce. You don't need cream, because it will be topping ice cream. What you do need is a sharp contrast to the cool creaminess of the ice cream, and that's what you get with this. The combination of chocolate and cocoa syrup creates a supersmooth, velvety sauce—and one that can be heated and reheated over and over again without sacrificing quality. It thickens but remains shiny and fluid on the ice cream.

The sauce will harden when cooled, and one of our favorite behind-the-line treats is to whip up some sweetened cream and fold in a dollop of cooled and hardened hot fudge to make a really good mock chocolate mousse.

Makes 2⅓ cups

1 cup water

⅓ cup sugar

⅓ cup light corn syrup

¼ cup unsweetened cocoa powder

½ teaspoon vanilla extract

3 ounces unsweetened chocolate, finely chopped

5 ounces bittersweet chocolate, finely chopped

Combine the water, sugar, and corn syrup in a medium saucepan and bring to a boil, stirring to dissolve the sugar. Remove from the heat and add the cocoa powder, whisking well to combine. Add the vanilla extract and whisk until very smooth. Add the chocolates and let sit for 3 minutes.

Stir the sauce with a wooden spoon or heatproof spatula until the chocolate is completely melted and smooth; the sauce will have a glossy shine when it is ready. Serve warm, or let cool and refrigerate. The sauce can be refrigerated for up to 2 months.

To serve, reheat, stirring, until warm and fluid.

HONEY BUTTERSCOTCH SAUCE

When this sauce is in my fridge, I find myself sneaking spoonfuls right from the jar. Cold, it solidifies, but it melts on contact. It would be a dangerous filling for a chocolate truffle. Warm, it's shimmering honey butter running over ice cream. It "butters" the

Sweet Corn & Black Raspberry Ice Cream (page 62; best made without the black raspberry sauce in that case), and is a wonderful accent for Sweet Basil & Honeyed Pine Nut Ice Cream (page 76), Ugandan Vanilla Bean Ice Cream (page 148), or any subtly scented flavor. It wraps the cake in our Gooey Butter Cake Ice Cream (page 164), which is just the right flavor with everything else there.

The flavor will depend on how dark the honey is and how caramelized you allow the honey and sugar to become. But, unlike caramel made just with white sugar, you can't judge only by color: the honey makes the mixture golden brown from the beginning, so it's hard to know when it's caramelized. For the most flavor, allow it to burn ever so slightly. But don't allow it to smoke much—if you see a few dark puffs of smoke beginning to waft off the surface of the caramel, quickly remove it from the heat and add the cream to stop the cooking.

Makes about 2½ cups

1 cup sugar

⅔ cup honey

1½ cups heavy cream

4 tablespoons (½ stick) unsalted butter

Pinch of fine sea salt

Combine the sugar and honey in a medium heavy-bottomed saucepan and heat over medium heat, stirring, until the sugar is melted. Then cook without stirring, swirling the pan occasionally. The mixture will become foamy at first, then the bubbles will turn to huge glassine spheres and subside into smaller shiny bubbles. At this point, the sugar will begin to brown rather quickly; it will darken around the edges first and slowly begin to darken into the center. Use a heatproof rubber spatula to stir until the caramel is a deep butterscotch brown, then remove from the heat.

Carefully drizzle the cream into the caramel, stirring until completely dissolved. Add the butter pieces and stir until melted and smooth. Add the salt and stir well. Serve warm, or let cool and refrigerate. The sauce will keep for up to 2 weeks.

To serve, reheat, stirring, until the sauce is warm and fluid.

● ○ ● ○ ● ● ● ● ○ ● ●

WHIPPED CREAM

One of the most important things to master in sundae making is whipped cream. Well-made whipped cream is one of life's true pleasures. At our stores, we whip the cream in a bowl with a whisk, 1 cup at a time. One cup will serve 8 to 10 people, so we whip cream many times per day.

A few hints: Invest in a balloon or piano whisk, which has more wires than a regular whisk; these whisks incorporate the air into the cream faster than a standard whisk. If you can find nonhomogenized cream from a local dairy, the cream will whip up faster and the whipped cream will have a lovely light yellow hue. And chill the bowl. The colder the cream and the bowl, the faster the cream will whip and thicken.

For some desserts, like Oslo Ambrosia (page 136), I like to whip the cream to soft peaks. For others, I whip it to a firmer stage so that it will sit on the top of the sundae or other dessert in the traditional way. And if you do overwhip the cream slightly, so it begins to turn a bit bumpy, just add a tablespoon of fresh cream and whisk lightly to smooth it out.

You can make whipped cream with honey or maple syrup. Just blend a little cream with the thick honey or syrup to thin it enough to blend easily with the rest of the cream.

1 cup (8 dollops) heavy cream
1 to 2 tablespoons sugar
1 teaspoon vanilla extract

Chill a large metal or glass bowl in the refrigerator for at least 15 minutes; it should be cold to the touch. Add the cream, sugar, and vanilla to the chilled bowl and whip by hand mixer. Use immediately, or refrigerate for up to 1 hour.

● ○ ● ● ● ● ● ○ ● ●

ICE CREAM CONES

These cones are very tasty, light, and buttery. You will need an ice cream cone iron. I have rolled thousands of cones in my life, beginning at my first job at Graeter's Ice Cream and continuing through to this very day. And I have trained dozens of our employees in this task. It's not easy at first, but it doesn't take long to get it right—and the mistakes are delicious.

You can use this batter for countless variations: cones big and small, cups, tubes (à la cannoli), and more. Fortune Cookies with custom fortunes are a mainstay at our shops to accompany our sundaes; see the variation.

Makes 8 medium cones
(4 to 6 inches tall and 2 inches across at the top)

2 large egg whites
¼ cup heavy cream
½ cup sugar
¼ teaspoon fine sea salt
1 teaspoon vanilla extract
1 teaspoon almond extract
5 tablespoons unsalted butter, melted and cooled slightly
⅔ cup all-purpose flour

Turn on the waffle cone iron.

Combine the egg whites and cream in a medium bowl and whisk to combine. Add the sugar, salt, and both extracts and whisk for about a minute to combine well. Whisk in the melted butter. Add the flour, whisking only until the lumps have disappeared and the batter is smooth.

Make the cones in the waffle cone iron according to the directions for your iron. To shape the cones, follow the instructions with the photographs on the next page. When you get really good, there should be no hole in the bottom of the cone!

The cones are best the same day they are made, but they will keep for a week in a sealed container.

VARIATION
Fortune Cookies
Write fortunes on 5- to 6-inch-long strips of paper (the snake tongue makes a nice finish to the strips). Set aside.

Spoon about 1 tablespoon of the batter onto the center of the iron and close the lid. When it is ready, follow the instructions with the photographs on page 205. (Makes 10 to 12 cookies.)

HOW TO MAKE ICE CREAM CONES Pull the baked round off the iron and position the roller across the middle, leaving room at the bottom to grip the point of the cone. Working very quickly, fold one side across the roller and tuck under the cone. Pressing firmly, roll the cone over to finish. Allow it to cool for a few moments in order to set. Remove and repeat.

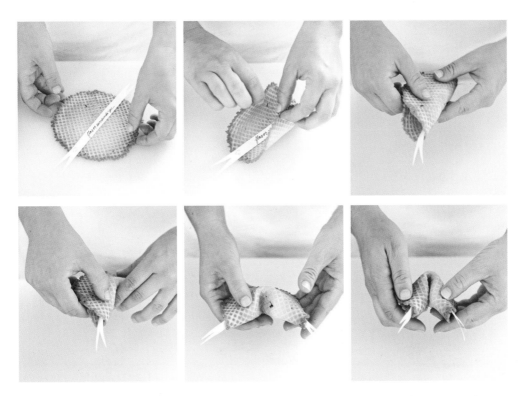

HOW TO MAKE FORTUNE COOKIES Pull the round off the iron and place the fortune across the center. Pull the sides up together and press. Crimp the cookie in the center, allow the corners to balloon out. Hold for a few moments in order to set.

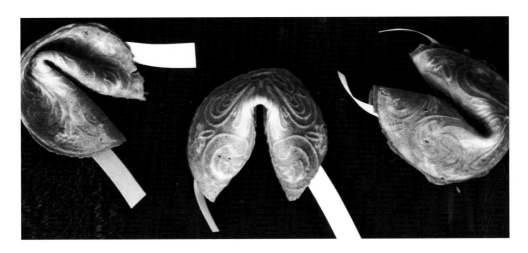

FLAVOR
IS WHAT SURROUNDS YOU

• • • • •

What is flavor? It's your culture. Your travels. Your history. Your interests. Your bookshelf. Your tastes. Your style. When you dine out at a restaurant or eat in an artisanal ice cream shop, you are entering the chef's or artisan's flavor world, full of the stories that she wants to tell.

Ice cream artisans come up with flavors the same way that you do: they begin with what is in front of them. In my case, sweet corn, hickory nuts, black walnuts, stone fruits, spicebush berries, strawberries, blueberries, red and black raspberries, Ohio cream—pure midwestern. Add to that my experiences in various places where I have lived and spent time that left a big impression: Miami, Puerto Rico, a small island in Greece, the South of France, northern Italy, and on and on. There are the people who have influenced me; my friends and fellow merchants at the North Market; and my heroines: Maida Heatter, Fannie Farmer, Julia Child. And there is my imagination: Marie Antoinette's table, Port Royale in the 1630s, Matisse's landscapes . . . all have inspired me. My aspirations . . . modern Melbourne, Patagonia.

Your life is rich with flavor. Look back on your own experiences, and read about other ones. Flavor has the power to transport (like a mini vacation) and transform.

SOURCES

• • • • •

CHOCOLATES

Askinosie (www.askinosie.com)

Valrhona (www.valrhona.com)

Green & Black's (www.greenandblacks.com)

The Ghirardelli Chocolate Company
(www.ghirardellichocolate.com)

El Rey (www.chocolateselrey.com)

Callebaut (www.callebaut.com)

SPICES, EXTRACTS, AND OTHER FLAVORINGS

NATURAL BUTTER FLAVOR
Frontier Natural Products Co-op (www.frontiercoop.com)

ALMOND EXTRACT
Frontier Natural Products Co-op (www.frontiercoop.com)

VANILLA BEANS
Penzeys Spices (www.penzeys.com) and Whole Foods
Market (www.wholefoodsmarket.com)

ESSENTIALS OILS
Aftelier Perfumes (www.aftelier.com)

PEPPERMINT OIL
Crosby Mint Farm (www.crosbymintfarm.com)

ORANGE BLOSSOM WATER
Mediterranean and Indian groceries

PIMENT D'ESPELETTE PEPPER
See Smell Taste (www.seesmelltaste.com)

VIETNAMESE CINNAMON
Penzeys Spices (www.penzeys.com)

MADRAS CURRY POWDER
See Smell Taste (www.seesmelltaste.com)

DRIED HIBISCUS
Frontier Natural Products Co-op (www.frontiercoop.com)

CANDIED FENNEL SEEDS
Patel Brothers (www.patelbros.com) and other Indian
groceries

CHEESES

GOUDA
Oakvale Farmstead Cheese (www.oakvalecheese.com)

GOAT CHEESE
Mackenzie Creamery (www.mackenziecreamery.com) and
Blue Jacket Dairy (www.bluejacketdairy.com)

SUGARS

TURBINADO SUGAR
India Tree (www.indiatree.com) and many supermarkets

MUSCOVADO SUGAR
India Tree (www.indiatree.com) and natural foods stores

NUTS

HICKORY NUTS
Integration Acres (www.integrationacres.com)

BLACK WALNUTS
Integration Acres (www.integrationacres.com)

OLIVE OIL

SINGLE-ESTATE OLIVE OILS
FROM AROUND THE WORLD
The Olive Orchard (www.theoliveorchard.com)

PUSH-UP MOLDS AND LIDS

JB Prince (www.jbprince.com)

ACKNOWLEDGMENTS

• • • • •

It is with the utmost pleasure that I thank the many people who assisted me with this monumental project. At least a million thanks are in order, but I will begin with my family. My husband, Charly, has been with me through all of the stories shared in these pages, and my mom spent a lot of time getting the stories out of me.

In addition to my family, without my in-house team I never would have been able to write and design the book I wanted to produce. The work of Casey Carmell, our graphic designer, is always thoughtful and full of energy, and it consistently reflects the spirit of our ice creams. In the book, her work simply shines.

Aaron Beck, Jeni's Splendid Ice Creams' copywriter, works closely with Casey every day, and he exhibited his great wit and a remarkable capacity to steam forward through the entire editing process. Aaron did his best to help me meet deadlines, and I am so happy to have him on our team. Many thanks also go to Joannie Colner-D'Andrea, who assisted on the first drafts of the book. Thank you, Billy Pietrykowski, my assistant. How did I ever get anything done without you?

Without recipe tester Christen Corey, I'm certain that this book would have taken another year to produce. Christen spent month after month in our humble little test kitchen helping to precisely execute every recipe in these pages.

Thanks are in order to every photographer who waited patiently for the perfect melt. The Midwest team included Stacy Newgent, who shot almost all the photographs in the book and made everything look so dreamy and pretty; the charismatic Ely Brothers; my good friend

Michelle Maguire, whose idiosyncratic work is always brilliant; and Lisa Fjeld, who came through when we needed even more elegant pictures. Big-time thanks for friendship and always-gorgeous images go to our Big City photo connection, George Lange. Many thanks also to Sally MacLeod for her skillfull illustrations.

Beyond the immediate squad that helped with the book, I must thank Kristin Donnelly (at *Food & Wine* magazine), who planted the seed for this book; Dr. Valente D. Alvarez, Professor of Dairy Food Processing and Director of the Food Industries Center at Ohio State University; and Professor Mike Mangino, Professor Emeritus at Ohio State University and an expert in whey protein denaturation, for verifying my theories on why this recipe works so well.

Without Columbus itself and its extensive network of independent-minded souls, neither this book nor Jeni's Splendid Ice Creams would exist. Franklin Park Conservatory, whose beautiful gardens inspire us throughout the year, granted us permission to shoot loads of photos, and our dear inspirational friend Yusef Riazi allowed us to shoot the cocktail photographs in his beautiful space at Mouton. The Upper Arlington and Columbus Metropolitan Libraries, where I often go for inspiration, were sanctuaries where we laid the groundwork for the book in the winter of 2009.

The insightful, hardworking, and dedicated people, farms, suppliers, and organizations that make up Columbus's food community include several I work with all the time, and without them I'd be lost. Among them are far too many to thank here, but those I must doff my cap to are chef Alana Shock for being my earliest and staunchest supporter; longtime friend Lisa Gingerich Dillman, whose palate I trust deeply; Michael Jones and the team at Local Matters, who are changing the world of food; our friends at the Wayward Seed Farm; Jorgensen Farms; Integration Acres; the Chef's Garden; and the North Market; and most important, our innovative dairy family at Snowville Creamery, which is led by Warren Taylor and Victoria (Mitchell) Taylor, Bill Dix, and Stacy Hall.

Beyond Ohio, we work with a handful of like-minded people I must commend, including Shawn Askinosie, whose direct partnerships with cacao farmers around the world yield chocolate with true flavor and heart; Ndali Estate's Lulu Sturdy, who inspires me so much with her disposition, dedication, and out-of-this-world vanilla; Dean & DeLuca co-founder Giorgio DeLuca, for seeing the potential of handcrafted ice cream long ago.

While the aforementioned people contributed greatly, no one contributed more than the team at Artisan. My publisher truly operates as a family-owned company, and I loved working with them. My editor, Ann Bramson, gave us so much freedom to write, style, and design the book, and we learned so much about the process. Trent Duffy and Kevin Brainard just might be the two most patient and persistent people in the publishing business, and they worked wonders to keep, or at least try to keep, us all on schedule. Also at Artisan, we appreciate the efforts of Susan Baldaserini, Amy Corley, Bridget Heiking, Nancy Murray, Barbara Peragine, and Judith Sutton. And thank you to my agent, Jonah Straus, for all that you do.

At Jeni's everyone takes ice cream seriously, and I couldn't imagine doing this without all of you, including our captain, John Lowe, whose leadership has prepared everyone here for the next things. Nor can I fathom doing what we're doing without my brother-in-law Tom Bauer, whom I thank from the bottom of my heart for getting the word out about us from coast to coast.

As for my husband, Charly, we could not have done this without each other. I am so glad all those years ago that we jumped off and never looked back. I look forward to all of the other great things we will do in our life together. For my daughter, Greta, and son, Dashiell, I hope someday you will be proud of your mama, because I am proud of you every day.

INDEX

• • • • •

ABOUT THE AUTHOR

• • • • •

Jeni Britton Bauer and her husband, Charly Bauer, founded Jeni's Splendid Ice Creams in 2002. Today there are seven stores in Columbus and one in Cleveland. The ice creams, yogurts, and sorbets that Jeni and her kitchen team make with fresh Ohio ingredients and exotics from around the world are available in an ever-increasing number of select groceries and restaurants throughout the United States and via mail order. Devotees who scan Jeni's Web site, blog, Facebook page, and Twitter feed daily cause a veritable run on seasonal flavors, sundaes, and other treats.

The flavors that make up Jeni's collections are inspired by the seasons of the Midwestern year. Regardless of the time of year, all Jeni's ice creams and yogurts are made with cream and milk from cows that graze grass on a farm one hundred miles southeast of the Jeni's kitchen. Not only does this partnership yield delicious, high-quality, artisanal ice creams and yogurts, but the union allows both companies to grow together with a focus on quality and sustainability.

Jeni's uncompromising standards, artful attention to details, and devotion to the science and craft of ice cream making were cultivated during work in a French pâtisserie, as well as during her studies at Ohio State University and Penn State University. Jeni's Splendid Ice Creams have been lauded by *The New York Times, Food & Wine, The Washington Post, Bon Appétit, The Boston Globe, Chicago Tribune, Out,* and *The Atlantic Monthly,* among others.

Jeni, whose own favorite flavors are Lemon Frozen Yogurt and Ylang-Ylang Ice Cream with Clove and Honeycomb, lives with her husband and young children, Greta and Dashiell, in Columbus, Ohio.

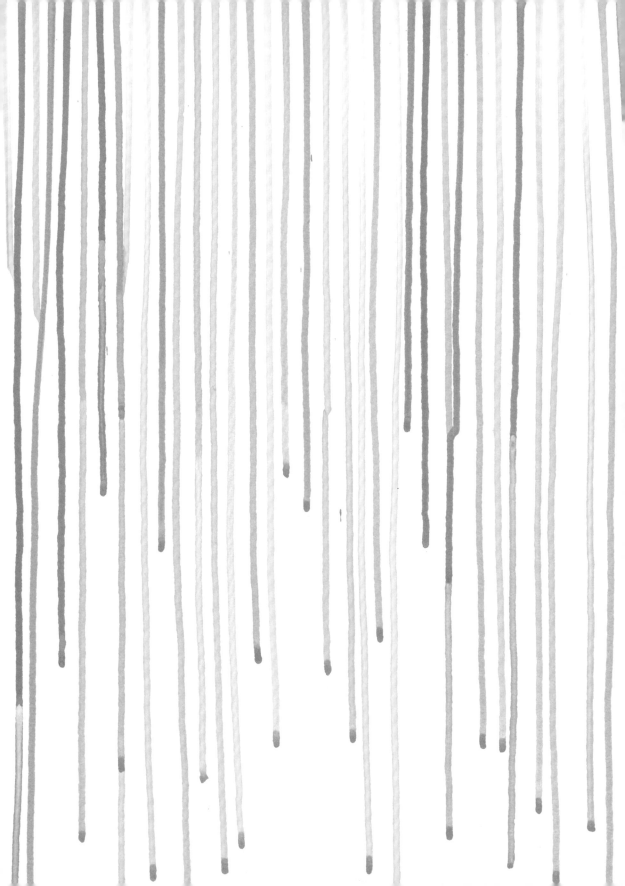

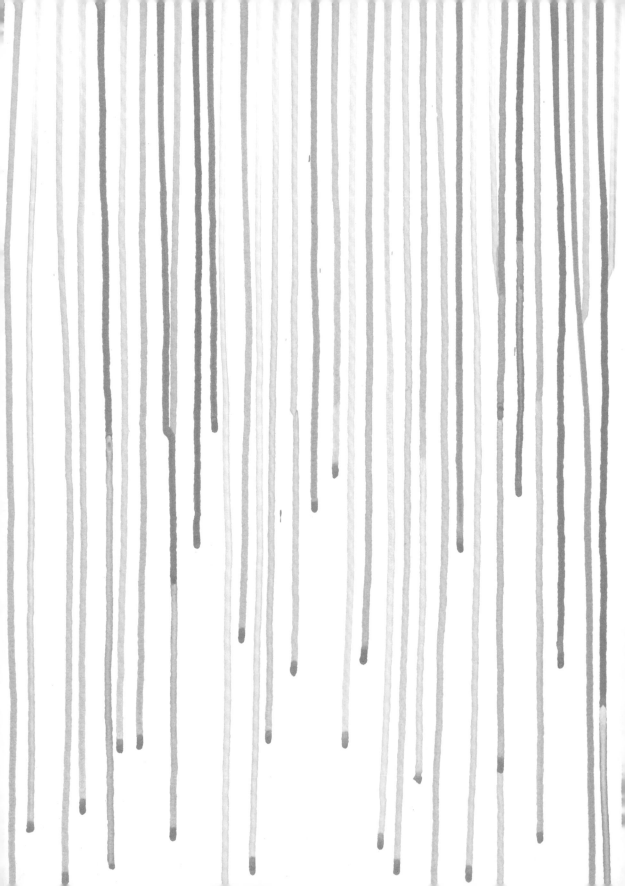